From H-Bomb
to Star Wars

From H-Bomb to Star Wars

The Politics of Strategic Decision Making

Jonathan B. Stein

LexingtonBooks
D.C. Heath and Company
Lexington, Massachusetts
Toronto

Library of Congress Cataloging in Publication Data

Stein, Jonathan B.
From H-bomb to star wars.

Bibliography: p.
Includes index.
1. United States—Military policy—Decision making. 2. Arms race—
History—20th century. 3. Hydrogen bomb. 4. Space weapons. 5. Ballistic
missile defenses—United States. I. Title.
UA23.S685   1984   355'.0335'73   84-47938
ISBN 0-669-08968-0 (alk. paper)
ISBN 0-669-09176-6 (pbk.: alk. paper)

Second printing, June 1985

Published simultaneously in Canada

Printed in the United States of America on acid-free paper

Casebound International Standard Book Number: 0-669-08968-0

Paperbound International Standard Book Number: 0-669-09176-6

Library of Congress Catalog Card Number: 84-47938

To Dan

Contents

Foreword

In the history of nuclear weapons, so many developments appear in retrospect to have been inevitable. The pace of technology and of industrial society made the unleashing of the atom only a matter of time. Surely the thousand-fold leap from crude fission weapons to the awesome hydrogen bomb could not have been avoided. Nor could any of the other technical advances, from the many-headed weapons called multiple, independently-targetable re-entry vehicles (MIRVs) to the Reagan Administration's recently-proposed Strategic Defense Initiative (SDI)—popularly known as Star Wars. Prometheus is forever unbound! The march of science, it seems, has a logic of its own. Mankind can only hope to deal, however inadequately, with the consequences of its inventions.

Yet this view has never stifled doubts about the major premises of nuclear arms. Especially in recent years, rising popular concern in the United States about the perils of the nuclear age has led to renewed questioning. It has taken several forms. As in earlier years, there are recurrent challenges to the proposition that particular weapons should be built. In the late 1960s, debate centered on ballistic missile defense (BMD) and MIRVs. More recently, the B-1 bomber and the MX intercontinental ballistic missile (ICBM) have been the focus of attention. Likewise, today the Star Wars initiative is just beginning to fuel new political debate. In each such debate, proponents have argued that the advance of technology would inevitably make the contested or comparable weapons available to the Soviet Union and that we should not be left at a disadvantage. Opponents have often conceded the point about the role of technology, while disputing the political arguments for acceding to its demands.

Questions about nuclear arms now also include doctrine and strategy: for example, the morality of the basic deterrent doctrine of mutual assured destruction (MAD) that bases security on holding hostage tens of millions of people; the idea that under some circumstances nuclear war can be fought successfully if deterrence fails; and the U.S. commitment to initiate the use of nuclear weapons ("first use") in face of major non-nuclear Soviet attack on Western Europe. Again, however, the premise that technology drives nuclear developments has gone largely unchallenged.

Yet more recently, growing popular frustration over the failure of the two superpowers to impose more than modest limits on the development and deployment of nuclear arms is also stimulating a new look at the role of technology. The debate over the MX missile, for example, has elicited deep misgivings about the wisdom of our developing MIRVs fifteen years ago—misgivings shared even by some former officials who had championed this development that permits a single missile to destroy more than one enemy city or missile silo. Would the Soviets have developed MIRVs even if we had not done so first? The answer no longer is unequivocally "yes." One alternative to MX—the single-warhead Midgetman missile—is in essence an effort to turn the clock back: if not to uninvent the MIRV, at least to purge nuclear arsenals of its inherent threat to the stability of mutual deterrence.

The key thrust of this new thinking—eloquently advanced by Jonathan Stein in the following pages—is that technology itself has not been the villain of the piece, nor is it today with the new Star Wars proposal. We have, all along, been substantially in control of our destiny. We (and presumably the Soviets) have chosen in our politics the paths we have taken in nuclear arms.

On reflection, this idea with its reaffirmation of free will should not be surprising. In the past, basic science may have marched ineluctably to divine the nature and potential of the atom's elemental force. But refinements of knowledge in nuclear arms today do not just spring from the minds of latter-day Einsteins or from rudimentary instruments in a Cavendish Laboratory. Even more to the point, ideas do not become weapons—either nuclear explosives or the means to deliver them—without capital investments of staggering proportions. The Manhattan Project that built the first atomic bomb was itself no small endeavor. This implies that no significant developments in nuclear arms will take place unless governments will their existence and devote the economic resources to bring them to fruition.

This is one clear message of the current debate over Star Wars. By conservative estimates, developing and deploying a system for destroying even a fraction of missile warheads launched in anger would cost hundreds of billions of dollars. Even then, the balance of advantage would still rest with an adversary nation prepared to make a smaller investment in confounding such a system. In short, there will be no Strategic Defense Initiative if neither we nor the Soviets make the massive commitment over many years that is required; and either could scotch the ambitions of the other with a new infusion of cheaper offensive weapons. As argued pursuasively in this book, superpower competition in the heavens would likely make the world a less safe place, following a needless waste of resources.

There is a critical second strand to the issue of technology. As a society, we have profited from the genius of our people and the productivity of our scientific and technical economy. Too often, however, we are misled into believing that technology can somehow be substituted for political effort and decision. This is certainly true in facing the dilemmas of the nuclear age. At times, technology has been a vital factor in making the world more secure from nuclear holocaust—for example, in development of the missile-carrying nuclear submarine that cannot be detected and destroyed. It is also true that, for the indefinite future, the United States must continue to maintain a strong and secure nuclear deterrent, although both weapons decisions and arms control agreements can severely limit the size of arsenals and reduce risks to nuclear stability. Yet there is a trap in pressing reliance on technology too far and temptation to believe that development of some new weapon will in itself remove the specter of nuclear destruction.

Star Wars is only the latest effort to harness technology to escape a nuclear predicament that at heart is political in nature and subject only to political resolution. To be sure, were a perfect defense possible, there could be little opposition to strategic defense. But even the strongest proponents of the SDI do not claim such potential success, and they must confront the reality that even 99 percent success would not forestall the possibility that millions would die from only a handful of nuclear detonations.

The Strategic Defense Initiative is about the future, but it must confront arguments that were made many years ago about the technologically more primitive efforts to deploy ballistic missile defenses. Cogent arguments were made then in opposition to BMD, and these culminated in the landmark Anti-Ballistic Missile (ABM) Treaty of 1972, perhaps the most successful venture ever undertaken in limiting weapons. These same arguments, spelled out in this book, hold true today and no doubt will in the future—barring the unlikely realization of today's alchemist's dream of the perfect strategic defense. There is déjà vu but with a difference: the imposing costs of Star Wars and an even greater hubris about the effectiveness of technology as a substitute for political action.

The Strategic Defense Initiative does stir deep feelings that there must be a better way of being secure than holding the world hostage. But as always, willing the existence of an easy solution does not make it appear. The better way may exist; but it will be found not in the laboratory or on the missile testing ground. It can be found only in the politics of the nuclear powers and in their collective wisdom and courage in denying the inevitability of nuclear tyranny.

Robert E. Hunter
Director of European Studies
Center for Strategic and International Studies
Georgetown University

Acknowledgments

I would like to thank the following people for their invaluable advice and comments: M. Glen Johnson of Vassar College, who looked at earlier versions of the hydrogen bomb section and provided several years of encouragement and wisdom; Dan Stein of Princeton University, who patiently explained to me the intricacies of the world of physics (and physicists); the writings of a generation of strategists, but most especially Bernard Brodie; my colleagues at CSIS, particularly James Townsend and Pauline Younger; and the many friends and associates who contributed their time and understanding and who are all, in large part, the source of inspiration for this book. The analysis within is the product of my own research while at CSIS, and therefore in no way represents the views of CSIS.

1   Introduction

It has often been said that the relationship between politics and technology is like that of the proverbial chicken and egg, or perhaps slave and master—usually political slave and technological master. In the nuclear arms race between the Soviet Union and the United States, neither of these formulations will do. The relationship *can* be sorted out, at least for the revolutionary changes in military technology.

I have chosen two decisions, separated from one another by a generation, to examine the question of politics and technology in the arms race: President Truman's hydrogen bomb decision of 1950 and President Reagan's decision in 1983 to attempt the construction of a space-based defense against nuclear missiles. Both were seminal decisions in the arms race in that their intent was to alter radically the nature of the military competition between the superpowers. The history of that competition subsequent to the U.S. and Soviet hydrogen bomb programs has been said to resemble a classical Greek tragedy in so far as fate has predetermined our shared destiny under which mutual hostility equals "business as usual." Are there applicable lessons from that history, however, that may offer a less tragic future for the next thirty years? I believe that there are and that they deserve at least some degree of probing *prior* to a national commitment that may prove strategically undesirable.

It is my contention that the answer to the following question—does politics drive technology, or does technological innovation and momentum determine (or foreclose) political choice in the initiation and solidification of armaments races—is unambiguously clear. In both decisions examined in this study, political forces dictated and shaped the outcome. Theoretical causation in all modern arms races seems to point in the same direction: politics provides the determining and sustaining impetus to genuinely new weapons development and acquisition processes. Again, the discussion is focused on quantum leaps forward in weapons innovation (for example, from fission bombs to fusion bombs or from short-range artillery to ICBMs), not on evolutionary steps (for example, from Minuteman I to Minuteman II).

That this is true is evident not only from an analysis of the hydrogen bomb and space-based defense controversies but from an examination of recent arms races as well: the turn-of-the-century battleship-building competition between the great European powers, especially Great Britain and

1

Germany; the development of the nitrogen-fixation process during World War I;[1] and the Manhattan Project's successful production of atomic weaponry in its race with Nazi Germany. Those achievements were the result of determined political processes in which policy debate preceded technological development and organizational implementation.

In 1976, Herbert York published *The Advisors,* his account of the hydrogen bomb decision and successive arms race developments. At the heart of York's arms race theory lies a firm belief in the prevalence of technology over politics. Two passages from his work suffice to demonstrate the foundations of his argument:

> In short, the root of the problem has not been maliciousness, but rather a sort of technological exuberance that has overwhelmed the other factors that go into the making of overall national policy.

> The possibilities that welled up out of the technological program and the ideas and proposals put forth by the technologists eventually created a set of options that was so narrow in the scope of its alternatives and so strong in its thrust that the political decision makers had no real independent choice in the matter.[2]

Through detailed analysis of the hydrogen bomb decision and through a preliminary assessment of the defense-in-space decision, it is my purpose to establish a challenge to the assumption that technological innovation or exuberance has foreclosed political choice in the initiation of qualitatively new weapons programs. The root of the problem is indeed maliciousness, if by this term York and many others are describing a set of nontechnological and emotional (that is, political) factors. Placed in the context of any modern arms race, technology becomes either a convenient tool to further organizational or personal ends or an invaluable aid in promoting a professed doctrine or strategy.

In some decisions, the policy pronouncement forces or channels theoretical research into unknown, untried, or unprecedented approaches. The hydrogen bomb directive is a good case in point. Thermonuclear reactions were examined for more than seven years before President Truman first considered the issue seriously. There had been little theoretical success and none experimentally. Truman's decision of January 31, 1950, for the first time focused concerted scientific attention on the hydrogen nucleus as a viable source of explosive power. The physicists, engineers, chemists, mathematicians, and statisticians were recruited from the nation's finest research centers and eventually attained Truman's policy objective.

That policy objective was but part of an emerging pattern of national defense decisions reflecting, according to Samuel Huntington, "the changing requirements of deterrence which, in turn, stemmed primarily from the development and expansion of Soviet strategic capabilities."[3] The postwar doctrine of deterrence led both superpowers to innovate:

> Innovation begins *when groups sensitive to the new need* take uncoordinated steps toward meeting it. In due course, the activities of these groups produce a "critical program," which assumes decisive importance in the minds of both supporters and the opponents of the overall innovation. . . . The critical issue becomes the focus of debate, requiring decision at the highest level of government [emphasis added].[4]

Writing on strategy and technology, Henry Kissinger notes "that both the development and use of weapons systems are impossible without strategic doctrine."[5] Particular doctrines, no matter how ill-developed or unsophisticated, inexorably lead to the development of new weapons technologies and even, as President Reagan is now attempting, to new and opposing doctrines. Because of the "inhibitions with respect to the use of force . . . the revolutionary contest between us and the Soviet bloc . . . [is transformed] into an armaments race."[6]

The notion that technology rules supreme is not a new one. Former Secretary of Defense Robert McNamara spoke of "technological exuberance" as the driving force in the arms race, a theme that predates McNamara in both the scholarly and the popular literature and one that has been echoed since then time and again. It is a theme, however, that is overdrawn. Discussing the impact of new technologies on the arms race in 1971, Jack Ruina of the Massachusetts Institute of Technology (MIT) states:

> Some writers refer to a "technological imperative" at work—that is, if a weapon can be made it will be made. There is no doubt some truth to this, but the concept is overly simplistic. There are restraints to the temptation to develop and deploy, without discrimination, the technologically possible . . . we did restrain ourselves from developing shipborne nuclear ballistic missiles, bombs in orbit, 100-megaton bombs, and many other technically feasible systems.[7]

In the past, a number of other feasible weapons programs, for example, the development of super-heavy warheads, was scrapped in large part for non-technical reasons. The United States, in fact, has not tested a thermonuclear weapon greater than 14.8 megatons (the USSR reputedly has tested a 58 megaton device).

Finally, the argument has been made that when one government responds to technological innovation—or in anticipation of an opposing government's innovation—technological pull is responsible. Is not technology, then, the foundation of the arms race? Again, the technology-pull assertion factors out the political dynamics that initially set both Soviet and American military-technological innovation in motion. In the Soviet Union, "military doctrine is expected to produce weapons requirements to 'pull' technology."[8] Political events dictated Soviet technological requirements following World War II and resulted in the first Soviet atomic bomb program, the result of which, in turn, initiated the internal U.S. government controversy concerning the hydrogen bomb.

In the pages that follow, it has not been my aim to remove the role of technological processes, nor to explain the arms race as a simple, single-factor analysis based solely on evil intent or political hatred. Technology is, of course, an essential ingredient in any arms race, especially after a race has begun or between various qualitatively separate phases. Technology is only one part of the Soviet-American competition, however. Its forward advance permits adjustments, modifications, and doctrinal attenuation but does not by itself dictate the essential rules of the game. Those rules were (and are still) written by political elites struggling to obtain their vision of strategic doctrine.

In an article entitled "Strategy and the Natural Scientists," Albert Wohlstetter discusses the "narrowly technological component" of such decisions as the development of the atomic and hydrogen bomb and the decision to use the atomic bomb against Japan in 1945. Referring to C.P. Snow, he writes:

> The cardinal choices, in Snow's sense, cannot be well made solely on estimates of the feasibility of some piece of hardware. They are political and military strategic decisions. Technology is an important part, but very far from the whole of strategy.[9]

2 Antecedents

Science has torn from nature a secret so vast in its potentialities that our minds cower from the terror it creates.
—Bernard Baruch, speech to the United Nations, 1946[10]

World War II ended one difficult era and began another. The nineteenth-century European state system, not fully destroyed by World War I, was finally ended with the defeat of the German armies in the spring of 1945. Soon after the Allied victory in Europe, a successful self-sustaining nuclear chain reaction was harnessed to an explosive test device at Alamogordo, New Mexico. The weapons subsequently dropped on Hiroshima and Nagasaki, totaling about 35,000 equivalent tons of TNT, were hundreds of times more powerful than the most potent "blockbusters" then in use. The nuclear age had begun, bringing in its wake exacerbated political distrust between the two strongest military partners in the "grand alliance"—the United States and the Soviet Union.

The race to acquire the atomic bomb began in earnest when the Manhattan Engineer District was created to oversee the bomb's realization. The famous letter from Albert Einstein to President Roosevelt in 1939—actually written by fellow physicist Leo Szilard[11]—aroused no great fear or excitement in official circles, although its import was clear to many scientists (especially the émigré physicists) involved in theoretical physics. The letter would not have been written at that time or with the same degree of urgency had there been no major rupture in European affairs. The warning of a *possible* technological breakthrough in Hitler's Germany convinced Szilard and Einstein that large-scale atomic bomb research would, unfortunately, be necessary.

The Einstein-Szilard letter urged a course of action beginning with theoretical fission research that would, step by step, culminate in a feasibility test. It stated: "It is conceivable—though much less than fission as a source of power—that extremely powerful bombs of a new type may be constructed,"[12] indicating appreciable uncertainty. Szilard and other scientific advocates of the potential fission bomb were motivated more by the exigencies of the war in Europe and the possibility that Germany might perfect the process first than by the state of the art in either theoretical or experimental physics. The birth of the Manhattan Project in 1942, then, resulted from the pervasive belief that Germany might develop the weapon first—a belief shared by President Roosevelt, Secretary of War Stimson, and General Leslie Groves (military director of the Manhattan Project). The impetus for the immense undertaking is best described by Max Born, writing in 1957:

> If there had been no war when the newly discovered fission process was being investigated, everything would have gone in essentially the same way, though somewhat slower. The first reactor might have been built five or ten years later, somewhere in the civilized world. The politicians and military would, of course, have got wind of the thing. But the difficulties and expenses of producing an atomic bomb are so gigantic that it may be doubted whether anything would have been achieved without the pressure of war. The Western parliaments would have hesitated to vote colossal sums for a project, the feasibility of which could be proved only on paper.
>
> The process was accelerated by a historical accident, as a chemical reaction is by a catalyst. The accident consisted in the fact that nuclear fission was discovered in Germany in the initial period of Nazi rule.[13]

A decade before the successful completion of the Manhattan Project, Hans Bethe published his work on the thermonuclear reactions of stellar interiors. Bethe shed much light on the fusion process—the fusing of hydrogen nuclei inside the sun's interior, resulting in the release of enormous amounts of thermal energy. During World War II, some incipient fusion research was conducted in universities and officially, in the United States, under the auspices of the newly formed Los Alamos Scientific Laboratory.[14]

Three prominent nuclear physicists—Edward Teller, Enrico Fermi, and Emil Konopinsky—were among the most active participants in the early thermonuclear research. Much time was devoted to the hydrogen bomb—or the superbomb, as it was called secretly—during a summer-long conference at the University of California–Berkeley campus in 1942. The conference was sponsored by J. Robert Oppenheimer, wartime scientific director at Los Alamos. The scientists were gathered ostensibly to discuss plans for the explosive design of an atomic bomb. Most of the summer, however, was spent investigating the theoretical possibilities of the hydrogen bomb. When the laboratory at Los Alamos was set up later that same year, the summer's theorizing about fusion was relegated to low-priority status in favor of rapid development of the fission bomb.[15]

With the focus now on atomic weaponry, Teller soon found himself the only physicist at Los Alamos actively pursuing the "super." (*Superbomb* or *super* was the shorthand term used to refer to the hydrogen explosive.) During the course of his research, he discovered "further objections" to the fusion work then in progress: " . . . and by the end of the war the question whether a fusion bomb, the hydrogen bomb, could be made or not was completely up in the air."[16] One fact seemed certain: the temperatures required to ignite a hydrogen explosion were of such fantastic proportions that the necessary heat would have to come from an atomic (that is, fission) blast. The fission process, then, was the logical prerequisite to the fusion process; in the future, atomic explosions would serve as a trigger to set off the much more powerful hydrogen bomb—should the hydrogen bomb prove feasible.[17]

Oppenheimer made it very clear after Hiroshima and Nagasaki that the small amount of work already done on the super at Los Alamos should be discontinued. A War Department memorandum written by an assistant to Secretary of War Stimson on August 18, 1945, reveals Oppenheimer's distaste for the potential weapon: "I understand from Dr. Oppenheimer the scientists prefer not to do that [superbomb] unless ordered or directed to do so by the Government on the grounds of national policy."[18] In a similar vein, former Secretary of State Dean Acheson wrote of the impression given him in 1946 by "Dr. Robert Oppenheimer and other colleagues in the Acheson-Lilienthal group that the hydrogen atom could not be cracked."[19]

Thus, sporadic probing into the secrets of the hydrogen atom produced few concrete results leading toward a thermonuclear weapon, because an atmosphere of concentrated scientific effort was entirely lacking in the United States. In Austria, however, Hans Thirring had made further strides in the theory of thermonuclear reactions, and the physical principles of fusion were now better understood compared to the pre-1939 research, although work toward a weapon was at best preliminary and halting.[20]

Between the publication of Thirring's work in 1946 and the initiation of the hydrogen bomb program in 1950, very few physicists devoted more than infrequent attention to the application of fusion theory to a practical weapon. The most notable postwar exceptions—Richtmeyer, Nordheim, and Teller in the United States—studied only specific fusion problems,[21] with little real progress toward either a feasible theory or a workable engineering approach. At one postwar conference held at Los Alamos in the spring of 1946, thirty-one scientists and engineers (including Teller, mathematicians John von Neumann and Stanislaw Ulam, and Klaus Fuchs[a]) were brought together for the express purpose of thinking through the hydrogen bomb's physics. Various options were discussed, and, by the end of the conference, a solution seemed within reach. The group's report stated that, despite inevitable complications, "simple modifications of the design" would "render the model feasible."[22] Their initial optimism was ill-founded, however, and the design submitted to the conference proved untenable.

The net effect of American thermonuclear progress prior to January 1950, then, was exceedingly limited and mostly unsuccessful. In the words of Norris E. Bradbury, the first postwar director of Los Alamos:

---

[a]Fuchs was convicted in February 1950, in England, of leaking atomic bomb secrets to the Soviet Union.

Now, it seems easy to say [sic] thermonuclear bomb has been developed by public announcement; it seems obvious that there must always have been such a device in the obvious cards. This was not the case. The state of knowledge of thermonuclear systems during the war, and thereafter, and *really up until the spring of 1951,* was such as to make the practical utility or even the workability in any useful sense of what was then imagined as a thermonuclear weapon extremely questionable [emphasis added].[23]

The reasons for the delay in the U.S. program were manifold. There were those who blamed Oppenheimer for deliberately impeding hydrogen bomb research. Still others believed that the fundamental physics of a bomb of thermonuclear magnitude was not sufficiently understood and that the technological component was too uncertain prior to 1951—the year in which a feasible weapon design was worked out by Teller and Ulam.

Organizational impediments and political pressures were also constraining research. The Atomic Energy Commission (AEC), created in 1946 and initially directed by David Lilienthal, was granted a wide range of responsibilities in the atomic energy field. All atomic-related facilities, equipment, raw materials, and personnel fell under the AEC's purview and jurisdictional control. The president set the number of bombs to be produced in the AEC's military program, and it was the AEC commissioners' responsibility to implement the president's bomb program: "Particularly in 1945, 1946, and 1947, there were certain fundamental objectives at the laboratory that simply had to be met."[24] Among those objectives were the stockpiling of fissionable materials[25] and the assembly of these materials into atomic weapons.

The AEC, through David Lilienthal's direction, believed that its congressional mandate required the commission to ensure the adequacy of the strategic weapons program as decided by the president. A quest to construct a wholly new type of weapon, it was felt (though by no means unanimously), would only divert the AEC from its responsibility to manufacture the requisite number of fission weapons necessary to deter Moscow.

After the war, estimates varied as to when the Soviets would acquire atomic weapons of their own. General Groves predicted twenty years, while the consensus within the physics community settled on a much more accurate four to six years after Hiroshima. The AEC's position until late 1949 (when the commission split over the hydrogen bomb's necessity) was a strong belief in the fission weapons program as the best deterrent to war in the absence of international control. Although the prospect of much more powerful weapons loomed ominously on the distant horizon, attempting a breakthrough in thermonuclear weapons before 1950–1951 would have been nearly impossible: "In the light of subsequent events . . . it would have been an error and mistake to try to hash about in a field for which none of the basic technologies then existed, and at a time when there were very clear things to be done in the fission field."[26]

In sum, the U.S. thermonuclear weapons program lay dormant during the first four postwar years. Physicist after physicist at the Oppenheimer security hearings (in 1954) repeated the same theme: "The program had essentially not been of any magnitude worthy of the name. . . . The program essentially did not exist except for Teller."[27] Against this background, it will be helpful to explore the prevailing climate of opinion in the United States in 1949, particularly within the policy elite, before undertaking an examination and analysis of the hydrogen bomb debate of 1949–1950.

3 Postwar Concerns

*But an effect can become a cause, reinforcing the original cause and pro-
ducing the same effect in an intensified form, and so on indefinitely.*
          —George Orwell, "Politics and the English Language"[28]

The causes and effects of the Cold War will continue to be the subject of
historical debate, but all will agree that at least some mistakes were made by
both Moscow and Washington. Numerous arguments have been advanced
condemning the actions of Stalin while lauding those of Truman, and con-
versely, with the particular analysis usually depending on the critic's politics.
Both governments, for example, engaged in massive troop demobilizations in
Central Europe; Moscow reduced its army's strength by roughly 80 percent.
Time and again, many opportunities were missed for clarifying misunder-
standings on both sides. One effect emerged from the politics of the early
Cold War that no one would dispute: the nuclear arms race.

The United States experienced the first stirrings of national insecurity as
a world power between 1945 and 1949. It is ironic, to some extent, that such
insecurity should have surfaced so quickly after the war's end, given that
the United States emerged as the strongest world power (with the European
provinces of the Soviet Union in ruins). Internal threats seemed as perilous
as external threats. Our "great ally," the USSR, had become our "great
adversary" by the winter of 1947–1948. Most Americans blamed Moscow
for poisoning relations, and a great many believed that Moscow was responsible for left-wing and subversive organizations in the United States and in
the colonies of our European allies. Was it not the oft-stated destiny of
Soviet Communism to destroy the *ancien regime,* the Old World capitalist-
feudal order?

These American perceptions of Soviet Russia did not emanate from or
flourish in a vacuum. The press and the politicians of both major parties
may have found lucrative political capital in exploiting threats from communism, but they reflected, in large part, their interpretations of Stalin's
role in international politics. The Soviet government did not bolster the confidence, trust, or amicability of the American people or their elected leadership. Eastern Europe was occupied by Soviet troops; civil war in China raged
with Soviet assistance to Mao's forces; threatening verbiage aimed at
Western Europe and North America continued where it had left off in 1943[29]
(when the Comintern was disbanded); and the ideals of the Revolution,

coupled with Marxist-Leninist slogans, signaled to the "decadent West" their imminent demise, to be replaced by triumphant socialism in the construction of a new political and economic world order.

The solidification of anticommunism and excessive national security concerns grew out of this mix of Soviet-American actions and rhetoric.[30] American policymakers became obsessed with security. The Truman Doctrine of March 1947, in which assistance would be offered to those free governments struggling with external interference from communist regimes,[a] won support in Congress through a major presidential address painting a stark picture of the incessant march of Stalinism. The Marshall Plan furthered the U.S. commitment to the political integrity and economic recovery of Western Europe. Finally, the Soviet blockade of the access routes to Berlin in June 1948 steeled American public opinion while officially dividing Europe.

There were efforts at reconciliation before the first Berlin crisis: the Foreign Ministers' Conferences in London and Moscow and the attempt to negotiate international control of atomic energy. The latter effort was an American initiative that placed the onus of refusal on the Soviet delegation. Moscow's reception of the Acheson-Lilienthal proposals of 1946 was hostile; the Soviets viewed the plan as a thinly veiled attempt to glean information about the Soviet nuclear program. Moreover, granting exclusive control of their nuclear reactors to an international organization dominated by pro-American states was unthinkable.

There gradually emerged within the American foreign policy establishment a political consensus, at the center of which lay the Soviet Union as an expansionist, aggressive power. Security policy in the United States branched into three separate but unequally weighted directions: restoring a European balance of power (by way of the Marshall Plan and later the North Atlantic Treaty Organization—NATO); internationalizing nuclear power, if internationalization could be achieved; and, more important, embarking on an "effort to evolve a force for two-way atomic war and a strategy to guide it."[31]

Following the Marshall Plan, Soviet perceptions of danger reportedly escalated to new heights: "The United States would enable and help her satellites to put pressure on or attack the Soviet ones, while American atomic superiority would inhibit the Soviet army from coming to the latter's aid."[32] For their part, U.S. military planners had to cope with a growing Russian army on the frontiers of Western Europe. The American atomic monopoly, despite its apparent potency, did not deter Stalin from blockading Berlin in 1948. Still, American planners believed that the military component in their three-pronged grand strategy would eventually prove to be the most useful—that is, reliance on strategic air power.

When the unification of the U.S. Armed Forces was legislated in 1947 (merging the War and Navy Departments and creating an Air Force sepa-

---

[a]The first recipients of Truman Doctrine aid were Greece and Turkey, whose governments were under military pressure from insurgents.

rate from the Army, all combined into one unified Department of Defense), it was clear that air power would be emphasized because of its projected decisiveness in any future military encounter. The president ordered the establishment of the Air Policy Commission on July 18, 1947, to report on the status of U.S. air policy and to make recommendations concerning aviation strategy.

The commission's report, published as *Survival in the Air Age,* carried great weight with Truman and with the advocates of a "seventy-group" air force. The authors of the report stressed the need to recognize the importance of enhanced security through air power: "Our military security must be based on air power" and "research and development must be increased" characterized the tone and direction of the report.[33] It proposed that a larger proportion of federal budgetary outlays must be channeled into defense and defense-related spending. Stimulated by the urgency the advent of atomic weaponry brought to modern warfare, the report recommended a state of permanent preparedness:

> It would be an unreasonable risk, and therefore, a reckless course, to rely on other nations not having atomic weapons in quantity by the end of 1952. It would be an unreasonable risk to assume that this country will surely have warning of the manufacture of atomic weapons by others.[34]

The makers of U.S. strategy fell into two camps, best exemplified by George Kennan and his Policy Planning Staff at the State Department, on the one hand, and the Joint Chiefs of Staff (JCS) and the congressional armed services committees on the other side of the evolving strategic debate. Kennan's once highly influential role was waning by 1949, paralleled by the rise of multiple centers of power in the Congress and at the Defense Department in the formulation of national security policy. The combination of powerful, conservative legislators and skeptical military advisors provided Truman with an attractive alternative to Kennan's politically vulnerable defensive doctrine of containment.

Kennan supported a strategy of containing Soviet Russia within its present sphere of influence through the application of restricted, partial, and balanced military force. An argument for a balanced force posture was a euphemistic device implying assignment of roughly equal weights to land, air, and sea power; it was one method used by Kennan to alter the drift toward overreliance on strategic air power and atomic weapons. Majority opinion in the JCS held differently, fearing that Kennan's limited approach would restrain manpower growth and hardware acquisition. The JCS also held serious reservations about war-fighting on a limited scale within the confines of containment. Kennan's doctrine would allow the Soviets to choose their preferred time and mode of attack and their preferred theater of operations. Further, as a direct result of these limitations on American power, the United States could well face its first large-scale defeat in the event of future hostilities.

The JCS plan called for a greatly enhanced air-power program, eventually providing the United States with the power to implement fully a massive "strategic air strike" in a military emergency.[35] The Joint Strategic Survey Committee (JSSC) supported the air-strike option over Kennan's limited-war preparations. Within the constraints of the budget ceilings (defense spending limits hovered between $11 billion and $15 billion during FY 1947 to FY 1950) and for the foreseeable future, the JSSC recommended reliance on strategic air power as the most affordable and militarily desirable defense policy.

In April 1949, the United States entered into its first peacetime alliance system—NATO. The Soviet blockade of Berlin had not yet been lifted, and Western Europe's governments had grown increasingly wary of Soviet intentions. A coalition alliance in nature, NATO signified the U.S. commitment to territorial defense of Western Europe and its adjacent sea lanes. Moscow's public reaction was one of outrage. Capitalist encirclement of the Soviet Union had been an important theme since the Revolution, and it now resurfaced after the signing of the North Atlantic Treaty.

Relations worsened appreciably. A sizable military-aid program supplemented the NATO accord (the Mutual Defense Assistance Program, approved and funded by Congress in October 1949[36]), leaving Stalin with the unmistakable impression that the West was now prepared to counter Soviet pressure, especially in Europe. Work on the Soviet atomic bomb, begun during World War II but not pursued intensively until after the war, must have been proceeding at a pace too slow for Stalin. Nevertheless, given the timing of the first Soviet test—several months following the NATO agreement—it appears unlikely that the new Western alliance alone could have stimulated such quick results. It is more probable that the date for the Soviet test had been set prior to the formation of NATO, probably after the spent fuel rods were removed from the Kyshtym reactor in late 1948 or very early 1949.[37]

With the rebuilding and refurbishing of both the Soviet and the U.S. militaries, intensive rearmament and the consequences of that rearmament became of vital concern to American policymakers. By the winter of 1949–1950, the United States was beginning to plan a comprehensive military rebuilding program, which later became codified as NSC-68.

The convergence of contrary Soviet-U.S. moves set the stage for the next round of bilateral competition: the thermonuclear arms race. In the last days of August 1949, the Soviet Union tested its first atomic bomb. Soviet science had ended the U.S. atomic monopoly. The response of the Truman administration, following the compelling logic of Cold War politics, marked the first watershed in the nation's long quest to achieve strategic nuclear superiority.

4 The "Super" Debate Begins

*The practical measures that we take are always based on the assumption
that our enemies are not unintelligent.*
— King Archidamus of Sparta, 432 B.C.[38]

In 1947, it was an acknowledged fact that no operable monitoring system
for detecting radioactive atmospheric debris was available within the U.S.
intelligence community. On September 16, 1947, Army Chief of Staff General Dwight D. Eisenhower ordered Air Force General Carl Spaatz to implement an effective monitoring system as soon as possible. A rudimentary
long-range detection program was in operation by the summer of 1949.[39]
Lewis L. Strauss, one of the five initial AEC commissioners (and an instrumental advocate of an atmospheric monitoring program), later commented:

> It is sobering to speculate on the course of events had there been no monitoring system in operation in 1949. Russian success in that summer would
> have been unknown to us. *In consequence, we would have made no attempt
> to develop a thermonuclear weapon.* It was our positive knowledge of Russian attainment of fission bomb capabilities which generated the recommendation to develop a qualitatively superior weapon—thus to maintain
> our military superiority [emphasis added].[40]

Toward the end of August 1949, several Air Force B-29s picked up
higher-than-usual levels of radiation over the Pacific Ocean. The source of
the radiation was believed to have been in Soviet Central Asia. Several days
later, government laboratories confirmed the origins of the radiation. More
detection missions were flown, and additional evidence was compiled. By
mid-September, there remained no doubt that the Soviet Union had exploded
an atomic device in the period between August 26 and August 29.

On September 23, 1949, President Truman announced:

> We have evidence that within recent weeks an atomic explosion occurred in
> the USSR. Ever since atomic energy was first released by man, the eventual
> development of this new force by other nations was to be expected.[41]

The Soviet atomic explosion triggered a momentous interagency debate that
lasted for several months, sharply dividing the advisory scientific elite, the
national security managers at the Departments of State and Defense, and
the civilian commissioners at the AEC.

Six days after the president's announcement, the general manager of the AEC, Carroll Wilson, told the Joint Committee on Atomic Energy (JCAE) "that no one yet knew how to obtain, even with a fission explosion, the temperatures and pressures necessary to trigger the thermonuclear reaction even if it could be triggered."[42] Commissioner Lewis Strauss testified before the JCAE that same day, warning that the United States was on the defensive after the Soviet blast and advising that we "regain the absolute advantage."[43]

Following a luncheon with Admiral Soeurs, then the executive secretary of the National Security Council (NSC), in which Soeurs asked Strauss "to prod the Commission toward a report to the President,"[44] Strauss seized this opportunity to draft a "Memorandum to the Commissioners." The U.S.'s relative lead in atomic weaponry was certain to diminish, he wrote: "It seems to me that the time has now come for a quantum jump in our planning (to borrow a metaphor from our scientific friends)—that is to say, that we should now make an intensive effort to get ahead with the super."[45] The AEC then formally asked its scientific advisory group, the General Advisory Committee (GAC), whether a crash program to develop the hydrogen bomb was advisable in light of the recent Soviet atomic success.[46] Strauss's memorandum is dated October 5, 1949. The GAC then scheduled its next meeting for the last weekend in October.

Scientific reaction to the Soviet blast was mixed. Oppenheimer (the GAC's chairman) and most of his GAC colleagues felt that Washington was sure to overreact, thereby unwittingly escalating the race to acquire nuclear weapons. Edward Teller, E.O. Lawrence, and Luis Alvarez represented those physicists who were less optimistic about Soviet intentions, and they actively lobbied for crash development of the super almost immediately after Truman's announcement.

The same day that Strauss drafted his memo to the AEC, Alvarez recorded in his diary that Wendell Latimer, a chemist at Berkeley, and he "independently thought" that perhaps the Russians were already hard at work on the super—and that meant that the United States must "get there first."[47] Shortly thereafter, Teller invited Alvarez, Lawrence, Ulam, and George Gamow to his home to discuss Soviet interest in the possible applications of fusion research. Gamow, a Soviet emigré and one of the most renowned twentieth-century physicists, related a personal experience that apparently resolved any ethical dilemmas the assembled physicists may have had. Gamow's story is related by Robert Jungk, a biographer of the early atomic scientists:

In 1932, before his eventual flight from the Soviet Union, he [Gamow] had referred at a scientific gathering to the work of Atkinson and Houtermans, in which, as was known, the fusion of light nuclei in the sun had first been suspected. After Gamow's lecture, he had been approached by Bukharin, the People's Commissar, who had asked with interest whether he thought such reactions could not also be reproduced on the earth. Bukharin had even offered Gamow the use of all the current generated by the Leningrad electricity works for experimental purposes a few hours every night.[48]

Clearly, the eagerness with which the Communist Party of the Soviet Union sought nuclear power generation and, very possibly, weapons as early as the 1930s must have been far greater by then, as the USSR would have need of such instruments in its competition with the United States. The physicists at Teller's home also believed that, given the Soviet outlook and the nature of the regime, it would be prudent of the Soviet bureaucracy to assume that secret military fusion research was presently underway in the United States.

On October 10, Lawrence, Alvarez, and Latimer met Carl Hinshaw and Brien McMahon (representative and senator from California, respectively) of the JCAE for lunch. McMahon was chairman of the JCAE and an ardent supporter of the super. The group considered the super vitally necessary for the nation's defense and thought it "might well save the nation from the Soviet threat."[49] The following day, October 11, the Policy Planning Staff met to consider further Truman's July 26 directive to the NSC, in which the president asked the NSC to assess the adequacy of the U.S. atomic program as well as the effects of accelerating atomic bomb production at the expense of other defense projects.[50] Kennan's staff met to reconsider these issues in light of the Soviet atomic capability.

• Kennan's logic ran as follows: If the military leaders continue to base all their planning on the strategic employment of atomic weaponry, the odds will increase tremendously that these weapons of *deterrence* will be more readily used in a conflict. Secretary of State Acheson added that if we agreed with the Russians not to use the bomb, "such a decision would make rather awkward a request of Congress for additional appropriations to make more bombs which we weren't going to use."[51] The breach between Kennan and Acheson was widening; Kennan dwelt on the tendency toward self-destruction inherent in the spiraling nature of nuclear weapons stockpiling, whereas Acheson was less concerned with theoretical projections and chose to concentrate his energies on how best to fulfill the requirements of the president's program.

The JCAE met next with the JCS on October 14. General Hoyt Vandenberg, the Air Force chief of staff, spoke for all the chiefs when he "strongly urged the development of this thermonuclear weapon."[52] In an October 21 letter to James Conant, then president of Harvard University, Oppenheimer wrote that Lawrence and Teller "had made the greatest impact on members of the Joint Committee and the Joint Chiefs." He also worried, as did

Kennan, that the military attractiveness of the super might be regarded "as the answer to the problem posed by the Russian advance."[53]

At the AEC, sentiment was divided. Lilienthal, Sumner Pike, and Henry D. Smyth were against immediate development of the super on both moral and political grounds. The remaining two commissioners, Gordon Dean and Lewis Strauss, favored rapid development. All five commissioners, however, were concerned with the current needs of the U.S. atomic energy and weapons program. Their immediate plans centered on three new projects: weapons expansion, planning for civil defense, and expansion of existing production facilities.

> As for the superweapon, the Commission wanted to know whether the nation would use such a weapon *if it could be built*, and what its military worth would be in relation to fission weapons [emphasis added].[54]

On October 19, President Truman formally approved a weapons expansion and improvement program, after a joint AEC-Defense study advocated such a step.[55] The GAC meeting was scheduled to take place in ten days. Because of the great uncertainty concerning the hydrogen bomb's development, the participants decided to wait to see the technical advice the GAC would offer. At this early stage of the policy debate, the principal decisionmakers were arguing for or against a hypothetical weapon that was not even theoretically assured on paper. Isador I. Rabi, a member of the GAC and then a physicist at Columbia University, stated during the Oppenheimer hearings his reactions to the Truman directive ordering the initiation of the hydrogen bomb program in January 1950:

> It was a very difficult question, because here is a statement from the President to do something that nobody knew how to do. This was just a ball of wax . . . we were really quite puzzled . . . there was some kind of feeling that here the President has given the directive and somehow something is going to appear at the other end and it was not appearing.[56]

Rabi was referring to the postdecision problem: *how* to develop the super. The predecision problem—*whether* the United States would actively pursue a thermonuclear weapon—had to be debated in an atmosphere of scientific and technological uncertainty. In a very real sense, technology was suspended from the deliberations. Only the vagaries of strategy and international relations and the political utility or disutility of the potential weapon remained to be considered.

5 The Debate Unfolds

And perhaps when they see that our actual strength is keeping pace with the language that we use, they will be more inclined to give way, since their land will still be untouched and, in making up their minds, they will be thinking of advantages which they still possess and which have not yet been destroyed. For you must think of their land as though it was a hostage in your possession, and all the more valuable the better it is looked after.
—King Archidamus of Sparta, 432 B.C.[57]

When the seventeenth GAC meeting was held from October 29 to November 1, 1949, the members of the advisory body were apprised of the meetings that had been held in the previous few weeks concerning the fate of the super. Their assignment was to examine the scientific and technical data and to render an official scientific opinion on the hydrogen bomb's feasibility.

The nine members of the GAC (with the possible exception of Glenn Seaborg, who was abroad during the debate) were temperamentally similar and shared close political views on nuclear weapons. They were not pleased with the emerging arms race, despite their key role in bringing about the nuclear age; yet they acknowledged, however reluctantly, the need to stockpile some number of nuclear weapons in the absence of an international control system. Should international control prove unattainable, then the United States must continue to arm itself to be prepared for defensive contingencies.

In regard to the super, the partial information available to each member convinced the GAC that this was a weapon the world could well do without. The GAC also knew that between the time Strauss wrote his memorandum and the convening of the GAC meeting, Oppenheimer's principal scientific opponents on the super—Lawrence, Teller, and Alvarez—had been actively lobbying the military and the JCAE to push ahead with a program. It was under these conditions that the GAC met in Washington to offer its advice.

During the four days of meetings, the GAC consulted with a variety of officials: the counsellor of the State Department; George Kennan, director of the Policy Planning Staff; General Omar Bradley, chairman of the JCS; Dr. Henderson of AEC Intelligence; Robert LeBaron, chairman of the Military Liaison Committee and advisor to Secretary of Defense Louis Johnson on nuclear weapons; the chairman of the Weapons Systems Evaluation Group; and General Norstadt and Admiral Parsons.[58]

Each of these consultants, representative of their respective organizations, brought a different perspective to the GAC meetings. These perspectives were not inhibited by a White House delegation. In this respect, the president and his immediate staff played the role of an indifferent arbiter—despite the president's predilections and acquired views about the nature of U.S.-Soviet competition gained from his previous four years as chief executive. Truman was not especially skilled in foreign policy when he assumed office, and he initially relied heavily on his close advisors in the White House (particularly Admiral William Leahy) and in the State Department (Secretary Stettinius and Ambassador Averell Harriman) and on communications from Prime Minister Churchill—all of whom were staunchly anti-Soviet in 1945.[59]

The experience and knowledge gained during Truman's first year as president stayed with him for the remainder of his term in office. A domestic liberal, Truman became an outspoken anti-Soviet leader. The pervasive effects of Truman's postwar anticommunism, aided by the Soviet Union's international behavior, greatly influenced the future pattern of U.S. politics. By 1948, it was political suicide for any politician to appear "soft on communism." Therefore, it was not surprising to find most of the participants in the hydrogen bomb decision possessing similar attitudes and assumptions about the nature of their enemy and the best way to combat the rising power of the Soviet state. Strategic air power and a superior nuclear weapons arsenal provided the popular alternative to Soviet blackmail.

At the State Department, even though Acheson and Kennan had long been convinced of the need to break away from a narrowly defined military interpretation of containment, the preferred course of action lay in the deployment of fission bombs. Acheson, a strong believer in the diplomatic utility of a powerful military, wanted an acceleration of the fission weapons program; he had been "unhappy" when the President fixed the upper limit of the defense budget at $13.5 billion in the summer of 1949.[60]

At the Defense Department, the uniformed military could not devote full attention to the unfolding hydrogen bomb debate, because the Navy and the Air Force were battling one another before Congress at the "unification and strategy" hearings (October 6–21). The Navy's attempt to quash a proposed squadron of B-36 bombers (the Navy wanted the prototype B-36 funding deleted in favor of a fleet of new supercarriers) turned into a heated Navy attack on the dangers of an imbalanced force posture featuring strategic air power.[61]

With the most important officers from the armed forces tied up before Congress, the Defense Department committed a small number of people to push the super's development. Secretary Johnson adhered to the JCS view that the super could offer greater utility as a deterrent than fission weapons could and that, in any case, it would be more useful in a conflict with the Russians, given their newly demonstrated fission bomb capability.

Johnson further believed that negotiations with the Soviet Union had proved useless in the past and could prove damaging in the future. He felt that the super "would have psychological value" in bolstering our deterrent posture[62] and that this was more important than a series of futile negotiations. In addition, he believed that the construction of a number of hydrogen bombs would increase U.S. dependence on air power and thus stave off the reappraisal of defense strategy that Acheson, Lilienthal, Kennan, and others had been quietly pushing for some time.[63] Robert LeBaron represented the secretary of defense and was in any case directly involved in the decision because of his role as chairman of the Military Liaison Committee, which was established in 1946 as an amendment to the atomic energy bill.[64] LeBaron favored rapid development of the super in a crash program.

The AEC and its advisory group were in the minority, then, before the GAC began its deliberations. Of the five commissioners and eight GAC members in attendance, eleven either were strongly opposed to the super or favored postponement of the decision. Commissioners Dean and Strauss were the only proponents of the proposed weapon. Following a meeting with the GAC on October 30—the date of the official GAC report—Lilienthal recorded in his journal:

> At present the issue seems to me fairly simple, and fairly conclusive: this would not further the common defense, and it might harm us, by making the prospects of the other course—towards peace—even less good than they now are. . . . There is no scientific or nonmilitary by-product—it is straight gadget making.[65]

As the GAC members assembled in Washington to decide their position, they realized that the positions of the State and Defense Department participants had already—though unofficially—been assumed. It then remained for the GAC to alter the bureaucracies' thinking by presenting the first detailed report on the super. As such, the GAC report of October 30, 1949, deserves careful attention.

During the four days of meetings, the GAC considered most phases of the U.S. atomic energy program: the costs involved in weapons production and reactor development; the possible yields of various fission bombs; and the time required to implement different programs. Consideration was also given "to developing atomic weapons for tactical purposes and building a reactor generating a large amount of free neutrons."[66] The committee advised against "high-priority development" of the super on technical, political, and ethical grounds. Requisite studies were not yet complete, and the large amounts of tritium necessary to construct the super would require greater reactor capacity than was presently available.[67]

The GAC maintained, first, that no one yet held a clear notion of how to go about building a hydrogen bomb. It was therefore premature to discuss implementation for *crash* development of the super. Further, reactor capacity had to be increased before the required temperatures and pressures could be combined with the proper raw materials to manufacture a weapon.

The GAC also presented its moral opposition. The members foresaw "extreme dangers to mankind. . . . We are alarmed as to the possible global effects of the radioactivity generated by the explosion of a few super-bombs of conceivable magnitude. . . . [This is] a weapon of genocide." Unquestionably, world reaction would be adverse. Moreover, the economic and military costs would most probably outweigh any potential benefits:

> It is by no means certain that the weapon can be produced at all and by no means certain that the Russians will produce one within a decade. To the argument that the Russians may succeed in developing this weapon, we would reply that our undertaking it will not prove a deterrent to them. Should they use the weapon against us, reprisals by our large stock of atomic bombs would be comparably effective to the use of a super.

> In determining not to proceed to develop the super bomb, we see a unique opportunity of providing by example some limitations on the totality of war and thus of limiting the fear and arousing the hope of mankind.[68]

The document was signed by James Conant, Hartley Rowe, Cyril Smith, Lee DuBridge, Oliver Buckley, and Robert Oppenheimer. A minority annex, written by Enrico Fermi and Isador Rabi, advised against development in even stronger language: "It is necessarily an evil thing in any light"; it would be wrong to develop the super on "fundamental ethical principles." The two advocated a worldwide "solemn pledge," led by the United States, to renounce the pursuit of thermonuclear weapons—even without "control machinery." As in the majority opinion, Fermi and Rabi concluded that the United States could rely on fission bombs to counter a military attack with fusion bombs.[69]

On November 1, Lilienthal discussed the question of thermonuclear development with Acheson. He wanted the secretary of state to raise the issue with Truman before the super's advocates could overwhelm the president. Lilienthal would have preferred to discuss the matter with the president himself, but the JCAE's deep concern over the Soviet atomic detonation preoccupied Lilienthal's time.[70] Lilienthal and Acheson did not want the president to be railroaded into making a hasty decision based primarily on congressional reaction or personal emotion.

Lilienthal agreed with the GAC report. He thought it was a mistake to concentrate most U.S. resources and energies in the direction of air power and nuclear weaponry. He wanted to find "some way to tie the renunciation of the Super to a broad statement of national policy, such as only Acheson or Truman could proclaim."[71] The GAC report provided Lilienthal with the scientific expertise necessary to challenge the claims of the super's adherents in both the science and the policy communities.

Senator McMahon and the JCAE, however, were not impressed by the GAC report. Several days after the AEC commissioners met with the JCAE to discuss the GAC's findings, McMahon told Teller that the advisory group's recommendations "made him sick."[72] McMahon lectured the AEC, warning the commissioners that war with Russia was inevitable. Our only sure defense, McMahon said, would be sole possession of the super.[73]

On Thursday, November 3, the Policy Planning Staff convened to discuss the super. Kennan began by stating that he felt that Germany was the key to settling problems between Moscow and Washington. A mutual settlement in Germany and eventual Soviet withdrawal from Eastern Europe should first be negotiated. Otherwise, he reasoned, if we ruled out direct negotiations with the Russians and then went ahead and developed and deployed the super, "wouldn't we [be] pushing the Russians against a closed door and demanding that they go through it?"[74] Kennan's question was not satisfactorily resolved, although there was complete agreement that the U.S. government "would have to start with the assumption that the Russians were working on it also." Acheson proposed an 18- to 24-month moratorium on the super, "bilateral if possible, unilateral if necessary," in which time the governments of both the United States and the Soviet Union would strive to accommodate one another on the outstanding differences between them. Should no agreement be forthcoming, the United States should proceed with development of the new bomb.[75]

The point of general agreement in the State Department discussion—the assumption that the USSR was *simultaneously* at work on the super (though in fact no U.S. program existed)—was based on a U.S. projection imputing offensive Soviet military objectives and hostile intentions. As an example of worst-case analysis (that is, proceeding from capabilities to intentions), it is surprising that Kennan did not strenuously object to this line of thought.[76] Despite this anomaly, Kennan steadfastly opposed the super's development.

On November 3, Lilienthal began to sort the conflicting arguments in his mind. A U.S. decision to renounce development of the super (referred to in his notes as x) had to be followed by a Russian opening of borders. Without open borders, he wrote, "nothing else can follow but suspicion, fears . . . and piling up of x and x^2."[77] The pro-super arguments, he continued, assume that war is inevitable in three to six years and, therefore, that the United States must have the super for a retaliatory strike. If war was inevitable, however, should we not then strike *now* "on some kind of rationale while we are still able to inflict damage on Russia at low cost to us or our European allies?" In addition, if one of the stated purposes in developing the super is the hastening of an agreement on international control, then taking one more step away from control would defeat our ultimate purpose. Rather, would not the Soviets read our decision to proceed as a "declaration of intention to go to war, if not actually of war?"[78]

Lilienthal's thinking on the super was thus aligned with Kennan's. The following month, December 1949, Kennan left the Policy Planning Staff and became counsellor to the Department of State. In his new position, he drafted a long "personal paper" to Acheson, in which he wrote:

> Was it really our desire to see atomic weapons thus abolished? Did we really wish to move in a manner that would bring us and the world closer to that goal? . . . There were two ways they could be viewed. One could view them as an undesirable necessity . . . a form of weapon we were obliged to hold because we had no assurance against its development and use by others against us, but the use of which we had no intention of initiating in any military encounter. In this case, we would of course not base plans for defense upon the presumption of its use. Or one could view this form of weapon as essential to our defense . . . and as something we would therefore expect to use deliberately, promptly, and spontaneously in any major encounter, regardless of whether it was first used against us. In this case, we would obviously base our defense structure on the assumption of its first use; and we would place ourselves in this way in a position where we would presumably not be able to afford *not* to use it, if war ever came.[79]

Lilienthal had flown in from Chicago to attend the November 4 AEC meeting. Commissioner Smyth declared that the super "provided an excellent opportunity to reopen discussions of international control." The odds would be much improved now, as the Soviets knew (or would soon know) that the United States was considering a thermonuclear option. Smyth believed that if we announced in advance of an international control conference our intentions not to develop the super, the Soviet delegates might persuade their superiors in Moscow that agreement on control would prove mutually beneficial.[80] Lilienthal was most emphatic, continually stressing the need for the public and the government to realize that atomic bombs gave us a false sense of security and that the hydrogen bomb would do the same, except on a much grander scale.[81]

Lilienthal had served for many years as director of President Roosevelt's Tennessee Valley Authority; now, as chairman of President Truman's Atomic Energy Commission, he was ready to retire. On November 7, he went to the White House to offer the president his resignation. Truman wanted Lilienthal to stay at his post until he could find "a suitable successor . . . someone who would let neither the Joint Committee or the military run away with the project." Lilienthal agreed to remain and promised to deliver an AEC paper concerning the super to the president before McMahon and the "Lawrence-Teller" group could "blitz" Truman into making a hastily conceived decision.[82]

Two days later, on November 9, Lilienthal sent Truman a memorandum on the super. He warned the president of the dangers of radioactivity, of the equally good Soviet chances of developing their own super, and of the marginal increment granted in retaliatory capacity over present fission capabilities (measured in square miles of destruction) by target date 1956. The super would not make the United States more militarily defensible than before. Assuming that the Russians would attempt to build hydrogen bombs, then the "possibility of delivery by ship or boat may make this country more vulnerable than Russia to this type of bomb since air delivery could not take full advantage of the unlimited energy release possible with very large charges." The arms race between the two states would be intensified "in a new way."[83]

Lilienthal, Pike, and Smyth all recommended "against the development of a 'Super' bomb at this time."[84] Lilienthal further elaborated on his position by adding a personal view, allowing the other commissioners to do the same if they so wished. He noted that production of fusion weapons would "diminish that over-all strength" derived from our fission bomb stockpile, for the AEC would have to divert scarce resources and money to a still uncertain fusion program. The U.S. deterrent could be adequately maintained with atomic bombs. Should we proceed with development, "it may well close the door on a continuation of our present policies for promoting peace."

Commissioner Smyth wrote that a decision to forgo production would be "a gesture of good faith and optimism." He added that "such a decision is more easily reversed than a one to go ahead full speed at the present time." Commissioner Pike chose not to enclose a personal view but believed, along with Lilienthal and Smyth, that the warnings of imminent war were difficult to credit.

Commissioner Dean believed that the arms race was prompted and sustained by Moscow and that the United States must stay ahead of the Soviet war machine. If a single weapon, such as the super, was known to have the power to "obliterate Moscow," then perhaps the Russians might be deterred: "The weapon might cause her to postpone an aggressive war. It is axiomatic in warfare that attack brings retaliation." Together, Dean and Strauss recommended a course of action similar in its first part to the advice proferred by Fermi, Rabi, and Smyth: quietly inform the Soviets of our plans to develop the super if feasible unless the two countries could reach an agreement on international control. Dean and Strauss concluded by arguing that, should their plan fail, "or if it is felt that the possibility cannot thus soon be exploited, then proceed, if the Defense Department concurs, with the development, and announce this fact publicly.''[85]

While the president read the AEC memorandum, Senator McMahon flew to California and then on to Los Alamos to be briefed on the super. John Manley, an associate director of Los Alamos and then executive secretary of the GAC, joined McMahon and William Borden, the executive director of the JCAE, on November 15. McMahon strongly disapproved of the GAC's advice, referring to it as a "suicidal response to a challenge by an immoral and implacable enemy." If the Russians could not be made to "behave," then the United States would have no alternative but to develop the super.[86]

Robert LeBaron and General David Schlatter later joined the briefing session. LeBaron was in complete agreement with McMahon; he believed that the super would extend, not reduce, the nation's security. That same afternoon, Teller briefed the group, telling his audience that he believed that the super had better than a 50 percent chance of success. "To Manley and others at Los Alamos, the statement was another example of the way Teller's enthusiasm for the Super ran counter to his judgment as a scientist.''[87]

On November 19, the president sent a note to the executive secretary of the NSC, Admiral Soeurs, authorizing the establishment of a special committee of the NSC. The special committee would advise the president on the hydrogen bomb proposal; it was to be composed of the secretaries of state and defense and the chairman of the AEC. A working group, set up under the nominal direction of Admiral Soeurs, included representatives from the Departments of State (Paul Nitze, Adrian Fisher, R. Gordon Arneson), Defense (LeBaron, Lt. General Lauris Norstad, Major General Kenneth D. Nichols, Rear Admiral T.B. Hill), and the AEC (Commissioners Dean and Smyth, Paul C. Fine).[88]

The work of this ad hoc group did not begin until November 28. In the interim, Senator McMahon, back in Los Angeles from his visit to Los Alamos, decided to write a personal letter to Truman. With the aid of William Borden, his executive director, McMahon composed a long argument in favor of the super program. He clearly would not tolerate a decision to forgo the necessary feasibility studies:

If the super would accomplish no more than weapons already in our arsenal, why single it out for special objection? If, on the other hand, the super represents a wholly new order of destructive magnitude—as I think it obviously does—then its military role would seem to be decisive. . . .

The basic question, however, is this: what happens if supers are aimed at New York, Chicago, Los Angeles, and Washington? Will we possess our own supers, ready to retaliate in kind and to throttle the attack at its source—or will we lack such weapons and suffer defeat and perhaps utter annihilation as the result? . . .

If the Kremlin believes that it cannot outproduce us in ordinary fission weapons, then its logical strategy is to excel in the thermonuclear field.[89]

A decision not to develop thermonuclear weapons would pose a difficult organizational problem as well. In effect, allowing the U.S. nuclear weapons program to stagnate at the level of fission bombs would place "a ceiling upon our military advancement; *for I do not know how the Los Alamos Laboratory would occupy itself, after a few years have passed— unless it ventured far into the thermonuclear field* "[90] (emphasis added). According to Teller, the reaction at Los Alamos to the GAC report of October 30 was one of anger. The majority wanted to press ahead in thermonuclear research,[91] perhaps fearing that McMahon's warning about the decline of Los Alamos would come true in the absence of a new weapons program.

The JCS met to file their views with the secretary of defense on November 23. Their memorandum stressed four major points: deterrence, flexibility, economics, and Soviet intentions. The super would deter a Soviet attack while simultaneously adding "flexibility to our planning and to our operations in the event of hostilities." Economic savings would accrue because the super would enable better "utilization of available ore and production capacity per unit area of damage." Finally, no one could assure against the weapon's development "elsewhere" should the United States forswear its production.[92]

On November 25, Lewis Strauss of the AEC sent his own memorandum to President Truman on the subject of the super's development. Strauss urged quick action while distancing himself from the GAC's advice of October 30. The GAC wanted to press forward with the booster program (designed to boost the destructive potential of fission bombs by one or more orders of magnitude) in lieu of a thermonuclear program. Strauss had no argument with the booster program but felt that boosting was no substitute for the super and that the time loss would be unfortunate: "The time in which the development of this weapon can be perfected is perhaps of the order of two years, so that a Russian enterprise started some years ago may be well along to completion."[93]

On December 3, the GAC met for the second time to discuss the super, and the members individually reaffirmed their opposition to the weapon. That same day, Under Secretary of State James Webb wrote an important memorandum, providing some further insights into the nature of Acheson's doubts about the weapon and into the department's approach to the problem. According to Webb, Acheson "is troubled about the possibility that a decision to go ahead would be interpreted all over the world as a decision that war is inevitable, and that *we* have reached this decision, with all its implications and effects on all types of future decisions."[94] The bombardment of contrary advice (that is, advice contrary to the majority opinion within the government) from Kennan and Lilienthal, two men whom Acheson held in high esteem, took its toll on Acheson's thought.

Webb outlined for the record the State Department view that the issues of international control and thermonuclear weapons should be kept "completely separate."[95] This was in direct contrast, however, to the stated positions of Kennan, Smyth, the GAC, and even Dean and Strauss (who advocated the super's development). It is curious that the State Department would not link the hydrogen bomb issue to international control, despite the glimmer of an opportunity to bring negotiations to the fore—thereby recapturing the "action" taken by the Pentagon. The State Department had a blatant organizational interest in fighting the super, but Acheson chose, instead, to give up the super in order to gain the strategic review that was later to become NSC-68.

The GAC sent four papers to the AEC on December 3. In the first opinion, Hartley Rowe set out the Lilienthal position almost verbatim. The super would lull the nation into a false sense of security and complacency and would divert scarce resources from the well-established fission program to the uncertain fusion program. It would also aid Soviet scientists in their super program (if one existed), in part from the inevitable dissemination of scientific knowledge and in part from radiation samplings that Soviet monitoring systems would obtain. The hydrogen bomb would also seriously undermine the "moral values" of our nation.

John Manley maintained that the military advantages gained did not warrant the cost involved. In the third paper, Enrico Fermi argued that, although the super "would have a peculiar advantage in destroying heavy structures over a large area . . . the number of suitable targets was limited, and the tactical value of the weapon needed further investigation."

Oliver Buckley stressed the need for additional research into the weapon's design, effects, and manner of delivery: "Careful research by the best scientists and mathematicians available would provide a sound base for policy decisions without accepting the severe penalties of an hysterical all-out development and production of a weapon of which we know little." The next week, Lee DuBridge added his strong opposition, stating that he was against the super on military, diplomatic, and psychological grounds.[96]

Within the special committee of the NSC, Paul Fine (of the AEC's Division of Military Application) drafted a detailed report entitled "The Super" (dated December 8). Fine concluded that the miltary value was deceptive: "Unless the super weapons were very large, the damage area resulting from their explosion would scarcely exceed that of the fission weapons which could have been produced with the same materials and facilities." In the Soviet Union or elsewhere, there were simply not enough targets of a size requiring the super's development to justify the expense.[97]

Manley's twenty-three-page analysis focused on technical issues, but he claimed to be uncertain of the ultimate objective of the special committee's working group. Was the group "to determine whether the United States should develop the Super, or was it whether the nation should build such weapons if they could be developed? A subsidiary question was whether, having decided to do the first, the nation could avoid doing the second."[98] Manley realized that the odds were stacked in favor of the super's champions. Despite the number of people who opposed the super—a significant minority—and despite the weight of their arguments, the more influential participants from the military, the JCAE, and the scientific community would, in all probability, prevail because of the scare generated by the Soviet blast. As Smyth had earlier predicted, and as Manley also knew now, if Truman approved a program merely to determine feasibility, the momentum engendered by positive feasibility tests would be impossible to fend off in a climate of worsening relations between the United States and the USSR.

In the week following Fine's analysis, the Defense Department members of the working group circulated their views on the super. They began their memorandum of December 16 by examining the consequences for the United States if the Soviet Union alone possessed the hydrogen bomb: the American people would become demoralized; the possibilities of Soviet blackmail would increase; sole possession could lead to "increased truculence" on the part of the Soviets; and their war potential would thereafter be superior to that of the United States. If the United States could claim sole possession of the super, however, then our deterrent posture would be improved. On a tactical level, it would force the Soviet army to disperse troops and materiel, thereby making them "abandon the source of their greatest strength, employment of mass." Finally, the super would provide economy in delivery, since fewer "units" would be required for an attack.

The Defense Department group urged immediate determination of feasibility (to be followed by testing for "an appropriate weapon carrier") and the concealment of this decision through Top Secret classification. If the announcement were made public, the Soviets would learn of our plans. The "Soviet group sponsoring development in this field" would then gain ascendancy should an internal Russian debate be under way. The impetus to begin a Soviet thermonuclear program, if not already begun, would then be very great.[99] Paul Nitze, then deputy director of the Policy Planning Staff, also wrote a memorandum in favor of feasibility testing. In addition, he urged that a reexamination of U.S. national defense policy should be undertaken afterwards in light of the success or failure of the super project.[100]

The special committee, its groundwork largely completed by the working group, met formally for the first time on December 22. The meeting between Acheson, Lilienthal, Smyth, LeBaron, and General Bradley proved inconclusive. Lilienthal carefully laid out his position to the group: "The fundamental issue was international control, not development of the Super." A workable control arrangement would ease our problems with the Soviet Union, thus obviating the need for the super. Johnson and LeBaron, however, did not see controlling nuclear weapons as germane. They believed "that the decision was simply a technical matter with no necessary relevance to the broader questions."[101]

At this juncture, the participants could not anticipate the technological outcome of a decision to proceed, but they could assess political sentiment within the senior levels of the policy community—especially the respective positions of one another and their relations, in turn, with the president. Truman greatly respected Acheson's opinion, but Acheson had not yet committed himself for or against the super. Louis Johnson and David Lilienthal were not as influential with the president as Acheson was, but it seemed increasingly certain that the secretary of state would be unable to back Lilienthal. Acheson was experiencing political difficulties at this time, the result of his unyielding support for Alger Hiss. Additional firmness and resolve regarding the USSR could well stave off what Acheson referred to as the "attack of the primitives"—a reference to those groups demanding Hiss's resignation and trial as a spy.

Regardless of the Hiss issue, it seems that Acheson had decided by that point to support a super program. The program would then allow Acheson the long-sought strategic review he had wanted to direct since the summer of 1949.[102] Of the three official members of the NSC special committee, Acheson would emerge in the best position. Lilienthal would get the defense policy review he also believed necessary, but he would be saddled with the super as well; whereas Johnson would get the super, which he wanted very much, but also the review, which he did not want at all.[103]

Acheson was also troubled by the international prospects of the United States, which he felt had worsened in the months following the Soviet atomic test. In October 1949, when the initial policy papers and positions on the super were evolving, the People's Republic of China replaced Chiang Kaishek's Kuomintang government. The effect on Truman and Acheson was profound, not least of all because they were certain that unfortunate domestic political consequences would soon follow. The Truman administration had now "lost" a state to the communists—and not just any state; China was the most populous country in the world and there was a long history of U.S.-Chinese relations centered on the desirability of Chinese territorial and political independence. Both the president and his secretary of state knew that this would be read as a gain for Moscow and a blow to the United States.

There were other problems factored into Acheson's discontent. When the Berlin crisis had passed, Soviet-dominated Eastern Europe and the western districts of the USSR increased their pace of military preparations.

Soviet ground forces in particular were readied to an extent deemed un-necessary by the Western powers.[a] The formation of NATO, catalyzed by Soviet actions toward Berlin, contributed to Moscow's harsher foreign and military policies. Stalin had taken a hard line since 1947, "a kind of recon-naisance in force."[104] His overly suspicious attitude toward contrived inter-nal and external enemies worsened after his seventieth birthday in 1949, as "decrepitude" set in and rendered the Soviet leader extremely paranoiac until his death in March 1953.[105]

Acheson was not alone in his perception that world events were not go-ing America's way. The specter of communism on the march intensified during the Berlin blockade, and many Americans interpreted Mao's victory later that same year as a harbinger of still worse calamities to come. Soviet-American relations seemed destined to result in military, and possibly atomic, conflict.

It was under these international circumstances that the scientific, mili-tary, and political advisors serving President Truman calculated the pros and cons of the hydrogen bomb. The decisive plateau was reached at the first NSC special committee meeting on December 22, although the matter had yet to be officially settled. Thereafter, however, the strength of the interagency movement to oppose the super's development was effectively exhausted, and with it the chance to engage in early arms control negotia-tions with the Soviet Union.

---

[a]In his *Memoirs*, Kennan maintains that estimates of "Russian conventional military strength" were "highly inflated."

6 The Debate Concludes

The great achievements of science . . . are only instruments by which men try to do the things they most want to do. —Franklin D. Roosevelt[106]

Several days after Christmas, 1949, Lilienthal and Smyth met with General Bradley. The attempt to persuade Bradley—and, through him, the JCS—did not succeed. Although the chairman of the JCS recognized the inconsistency between U.S. development of the super and the UN nuclear weapons control plans, he felt that there was "no other military way."[107] Discouraged, Lilienthal "suggested the United States should withdraw its proposal for international control and admit the nation was in a nuclear arms race with the Soviet Union."[108]

In early January 1950, a steady stream of information concerning the super began to appear in the press. As early as November 1, 1949, Senator Edwin C. Johnson (Democrat from Colorado), a member of the JCAE, had indiscreetly announced on television that, in addition to the booster program, the United States had made "considerable progress" on a super weapon a thousand times more powerful than the blast at Nagasaki.[109] (Senator Johnson's interview on November 1 did not receive widespread newspaper coverage until November 18.) Johnson was in error, however, because *no* progress had been made on the super, except indirectly in the form of some improvements in calculating machines. Following the Johnson leak, several newspaper stories were written about the super, including an important article by James Reston of the *New York Times* in mid-January 1950.[110]

The day of the Reston story (January 17), the new director of the Policy Planning Staff—Paul Nitze—advised Secretary Acheson to proceed with the feasibility program but to defer stockpiling of the new weapon if it should prove workable.[111] The next day, Lawrence R. Hafstad, the AEC's director of reactor development, briefed the JCAE on methods of delivery and on tritium production: "The Committee's frequent references to possible costs of tritium production and talk about a 'crash' effort suggests an assumption on the Hill that development of the Super was already an accepted fact."[112]

General Bradley and LeBaron briefed the JCAE on January 20. The JCAE needed no further prodding; most committee members were fully committed to the production of supers, despite the lingering uncertainty on the part of some of the members concerning the bomb's feasibility. Senator

McMahon, as the JCAE's chairman, "volunteered the opinion that Oppenheimer and his associates had gone far beyond their area of competence in opposing the Super on moral and political grounds and for that transgression they would suffer in the judgment of history."[113]

At the State Department, R. Gordon Arneson was responsible for directing the Acheson position for the NSC special committee. Arneson advised that the president should be directed to order feasibility tests publicly to determine whether the hydrogen bomb was more than a theoretical possibility. At the same time, the State and Defense Departments should undertake a full-scale review of strategic policy, while the Defense Department worked concurrently on problems related to ordnance and carrier development. A deferment on quantity production was advised until the State-Defense review was completed.[114]

That review was later to emerge as NSC-68, one of the most important postwar defense documents urging rapid rearmament. The NSC approved the review on January 5,[115] but it was not actively begun until the Truman directive of January 31 was issued, concerning the decision to proceed with the super.

Lilienthal met with Acheson again on January 26. If the United States were to seek a more powerful bomb, he argued, would not such a perilous course "confirm [the] present wrong policy: that big bombs offer assurance of military security when none exists?" Despite Acheson's agreement, he felt that the international situation had deteriorated sufficiently in the past two years to justify the super's development. Before 1947, the secretary said, "we were winning." Now, with the revolution in China, the United States had been weakened. Mao's victory, he continued, was our "partial undoing." Acheson then refuted Webb's position that the international control plan be kept separate from new developments in nuclear weaponry. From now on, he stated, the atom must be "part of [an] overall settlement."[116]

The anti-super group unequivocally lost its battle on January 27. In testimony before the JCAE, Lilienthal aired the AEC's majority opinion (against development) one last time. Commissioners Dean and Strauss allied themselves with the JCAE. Noted scientist Harold Urey and the influential Bernard Baruch announced their support for the project, as did Representative Carl Vinson and Senator H. Styles Bridges of the House and Senate Armed Services Committees. So, also, did the Weapons Systems Evaluation Group, the JCS, and the AEC's director of military application, Colonel James McCormack. Each added support to the growing enthusiasm for the still hypothetical weapon. That afternoon, when the JCAE completed its hearings with the AEC, Truman told Lilienthal that everyone will be "demanding action," and soon.[117]

At his press conference that day (January 27), President Truman acknowledged that the H-bomb issue was under consideration.[118] Earlier that day, Truman was informed that Klaus Fuchs had been arrested in London and had confessed to passing nuclear weapons secrets to the Soviet Union.[119] Fuchs had participated in the wartime Manhattan project and had attended the 1946 Los Alamos conference on the super. The news of his arrest added to the pressure to make an immediate decision.

On Tuesday morning, January 31, the NSC special committee met for the second and final time in Admiral Leahy's office in the old State Department building to coordinate their advice on the fate of the super. In attendance were Acheson, Lilienthal, Johnson, Smyth, LeBaron, General James H. Burns, Adrian Fisher, Gordon Arneson, Under Secretary of State Stephen Early, Admiral Soeurs, and Soeurs's replacement, James Lay.

Lilienthal insisted that the issue at hand was not the super but, rather, the direction of the nation's foreign policy in regard to atomic energy and nuclear weapons: "To proceed forthwith was to miss perhaps the last opportunity to reexamine and realign policy so that American security might be based upon something better than a headlong rush into war with weapons of mass destruction."[120] The hydrogen bomb, according to Lilienthal, would magnify the weaker aspects of our defense program by acknowledging U.S. inability to deter the Soviets in Western Europe with fission bombs. The super's development would also weaken our public statements that war with the USSR is not inevitable or even likely in the near future, he concluded.[121] Acheson agreed with Lilienthal's outline, but he could see no other alternative but to proceed. The pressure from Congress and the public was increasing, and with this the Secretary of Defense readily agreed.[122]

Johnson had scheduled an appointment with Truman for 12:30 p.m., so the special committee decided to use that time to offer their recommendation to the president. A statement was drawn up for use by Truman. Lilienthal suggested "that the President's direction related to *continuing* work, rather than give the impression of suddenly beginning something wholly new,"[123] which is precisely what they were doing. The special committee had originally drafted a four-paragraph text; the third and most important paragraph read as follows:

> Accordingly, the Atomic Energy Commission has been directed to continue with the development of all forms of atomic weapons. This work includes a project looking toward a test of the feasibility of the hydrogen bomb.[124]

The original wording implied the lack of an established military program or prior concentrated effort in the field of militarily applicable fusion research. A change in the draft deliberately strengthened the impression that a substantial degree of effort had already been undertaken on the super, which was clearly not the case:

> It is part of my responsibility as Commander-in-Chief of the Armed Forces to see to it that our country is able to defend itself against any possible aggressor. Accordingly, I have directed the Atomic Energy Commission *to continue* its work on all forms of atomic weapons, *including the so-called hydrogen or superbomb*. Like all other work in the field of atomic weapons, *it is being* and will be carried forward on a basis consistent with the overall objectives of our program for peace and security. This we shall continue to do until a satisfactory plan for international control of atomic energy is achieved. We shall also continue to examine all those factors that affect our program for peace and this country's security [emphasis added].[125]

Instead of mentioning feasibility testing, as in the first draft, the final text refers to work under way as if it were near completion (or as if there were a realistic degree of scientific familiarity with the weapon).

Teller recorded his amazement at the language of the president's announcement. The impression was given, he said:

> that we could produce a hydrogen bomb by tightening a few last screws. People understood from this announcement that the job was almost done. Actually, work had not begun. We had eight years of thermonuclear fantasies, theories, and calculations behind us; but we had established no connection between theory and reality. We needed a thermonuclear test.[126]

In the president's office, the three principal members of the NSC special committee (as well as Soeurs and Lay) handed Truman the final, revised draft. Truman reiterated in private the position he had always taken in public: "that our whole purpose was peace; that he didn't believe we would ever use them but we had to go on and make them because of the way the Russians were behaving," and that "we had no other course." Everyone was in a stir since Senator Johnson "made that unfortunate remark about the superbomb." If not for that leak, the president continued, the quiet review of strategic policy that Acheson and Lilienthal called for could have been conducted in a less hasty fashion.[127] Now the policy reexamination would have to occur simultaneously with, instead of prior to, the attempt to build a super.

Colonel McCormack at the AEC had already contacted Norris Bradbury, director of administration and research at Los Alamos, in anticipation of the president's decision. McCormack directed Bradbury "to proceed at once with the plan."[128] There was not much that Bradbury could do, however, apart from beginning the process of recruiting a cadre of physicists from around the country to assist in the new fusion weapons program.

Following the president's announcement to the press, Truman drafted a short message to the secretary of state. In it he directed the secretaries of state and defense "to undertake a re-examination of our objectives in peace and war and of the effect of these objectives on our strategic plans, in the light of the probable fission bomb capability of the Soviet Union."[129] The directive partially allayed Lilienthal's concern about the nuclearization of U.S. defense policy. The Defense Department would have the hydrogen bomb, if it was to be had, but they would also receive a strategic review that seemingly would force the military into a more balanced defense posture. The roles of both atomic and hydrogen bombs would be carefully analyzed, and the doctrines governing their deployment and use would be clearly delineated.

The January 31, 1950, directive served as a compromise between the members of the NSC special committee. Though unhappy with the decision, Lilienthal freely attached his name to the recommendation, in recognition of the political forces aligned against him. Johnson did not want a defense review (in part because he feared it would bring about requirements that would demand more force balance and greater defense spending, to which he remained steadfastly opposed), but he, too, realized that the super could not be gained unconditionally. As mentioned earlier, Acheson was far more intent on his strategic review than he was on fighting the super.

Several days after Truman's January 31 announcement and subsequent directive, Senator McMahon addressed the Senate. He described the hydrogen bomb as a weapon nearly ready for production.[130] In fact:

> The bomb was an idea, tentative and glimmering—its theory based on bold thought reaching to the stars, and its slender stock of data largely unconfirmed by laboratory experiment. Despite McMahon's confidence, there was no assurance that Los Alamos could produce a thermonuclear weapon.[131]

George Kennan, still protesting the decision, drafted a Counsellor's memorandum on February 17. Referring to Russian intentions, he wrote:

> The idea of their threatening people with the H-bomb and bidding them "sign on the dotted line or else" is thus far solely of our own manufacture. And there are no grounds for concluding that the Russians, who do not require the mass destruction weapons for the establishment of an adequate military posture, are necessarily insincere in their stated desire to see them effectively proscribed from the conduct of warfare.[132]

If the objective of the Soviet leadership in 1950 was indeed the eventual domination of all Europe, then, following Kennan's logic, it would appear plausible that the removal of nuclear weapons from all national stockpiles might well have been their preferred strategy. The large Soviet conventional military advantage would leave Moscow in the strongest position on the Continent, no longer deterred by American nuclear forces. One could have accepted Kennan's argument, however, while still supporting the super. In fact, at a time when Soviet conventional forces enjoyed numerical superiority and greater proximity to the suggested theater of operations (Western Europe), only a qualitatively advanced deterrent would have appeared as a satisfactory counterweight. It is also unclear whether Stalin actually thought that the control of Europe was a realizable goal, in which case nuclear weapons would serve his purposes quite well within his sphere of influence.

Bradbury, Smyth, and the members of the Military Liaison Committee met at Los Alamos on February 23 to discuss the possibilities for the super's development. Thus far, the Los Alamos laboratory had not made any progress. Deuterium was available in quantity, extracted from water through isotope separation. The requisite temperatures, however—400 million degrees and higher—would have to be reached to achieve the fusion of deuterium. Those temperatures were higher than any reached previously through prior fission explosions. The fusion of tritium and deuterium could yield a fusion reaction at a temperature lower than 400 + million degrees, but "the uncertainties were staggering." Bradbury "thought that those working on the atomic bomb in 1940 were more sure of success than those now embarking on the quest for a thermonuclear weapon." (If Bradbury was referring to the American effort in 1940, he was surely making reference to theoretical studies only.) The difficulties lay not only in the engineering design but equally in the theoretical aspects of the problem.[133]

Secretary of Defense Johnson sent a short note to the president on February 24. He stated that, after full consideration, the JCS and he were "of the opinion that it is incumbent upon the United States to proceed forthwith on an all-out program of bomb development if we are not to be placed in a potentially disastrous position with respect to the comparative potentialities of our most probable enemies and ourselves."[134]

By the end of February, the original decision of January 31 was being circumvented. The military could not prevent Acheson's strategic review, but they could assure against the loss of additional time if they persuaded the president to make an early choice on quantity production—before the feasibility tests had begun. A decision on quantity production prior to experimentation would prevent another heated policy debate concerning production and deployment *after* feasibility testing.

The final report by the special committee of the NSC was dated March 9, 1950. Commissioner Pike had replaced Lilienthal as acting chairman of the AEC in mid-February, but the March 9 paper was largely a Defense Department draft. The brief memorandum covered expenses, probable test dates, necessary materials ("bomb quality U-235" for testing and for tritium production), and a final warning on the uncertainty of the fusion process:

Unlike the situation with the Manhattan District in 1942, when it was fairly clear that the process would work, it is simply not known whether the thermonuclear process will work at all or under what conditions. Time estimates are therefore nearly futile.

The recommendations were as follows:

a. Approve the program for the test of the feasibility of a thermonuclear weapon and the necessary ordnance and carrier developments, as now envisaged by the Atomic Energy Commission and the Department of Defense. . . .

b. Further instruct the Atomic Energy Commission to make preparations for the production of thermonuclear weapons to the extent necessary to avoid delay between the determination of feasibility and the start of possible weapon production . . . the scale and rate of effort to be determined jointly by the Atomic Energy Commission and the Department of Defense.[135]

Truman accepted the report's recommendations the following day, March 10. Work was under way on the strategic policy review, and Truman felt secure in the knowledge that an integrated study would shake up the military and force them to concentrate their efforts more on the USSR than on each other. The "fundamental design" of the Soviet adversary disturbed President Truman, however. He perceived Russian designs as "a world dominated by the Kremlin. Whether we like it or not, this makes the United States the principal target of the Kremlin—the enemy that must be destroyed or subverted before the Soviets can achieve their goal."[136] Therefore, to safeguard the security of the nation, Truman declared on March 10 that the hydrogen bomb research was "of the highest urgency"; he ordered the AEC to plan for "quantity production of thermonuclear materials, and approved a feasibility test of thermonuclear principles."[137]

The decision of January 31, 1950, was momentous because it led to the first thermonuclear explosion on November 1, 1952, and to the historic policy review completed in April 1950 (NSC-68). In the spring of 1951, some fifteen months after the presidential directive, Edward Teller made "a brilliant discovery," and, with the help of Stanislaw Ulam, ultimately arrived at a thermonuclear solution.[138] The first test of a largely fusion explosion (it was not a "pure" fusion but rather a fusion-fission hybrid) could then proceed.

The other result of the January 31 decision was NSC-68. The report was issued in two parts, one on April 7 and one on April 12, 1950. The lengthy policy study called for increased expenditures in national defense. It urged the U.S. conventional capabilities be greatly upgraded and expanded. Nuclear weapons deserved rapid production, but it was "imperative to increase as rapidly as possible our general air, ground, and sea strength and that of our allies to a point where we are militarily not so heavily dependent on atomic weapons."[139] Kennan and Lilienthal would have approved of at least this preliminary movement toward a more balanced strategy.

In a war with the Soviet Union, however, NSC-68 paid homage to the importance of "overwhelming atomic superiority" in deterring the USSR from using its smaller stock of nuclear weapons. Based on the military and political analysis of Soviet intentions and capabilities, the State Department authors of NSC-68 (primarily Acheson, Nitze, and the Policy Planning Staff) warned that the United States must be prepared to meet a variety of future military contingencies. As for the hydrogen bomb, the report advised "that we should produce and stockpile thermonuclear weapons *in the event they prove feasible* and would add significantly to our net capability"[140] (emphasis added). Less than three months after the report was filed, the Korean War broke out. The war provided the necessary "contingency" that NSC-68 discussed. In consequence, the military budget and related national security funding rose from $22.3 billion in FY 1951 (altered from the planned July 1949 approval of $13.5 billion) to $44 billion in FY 1952 and $50.4 billion in FY 1953.[141]

The NSC-68 program, saved from obscurity by the Korean War, was partially dismantled by the Eisenhower administration, not in terms of defense spending but in terms of the balanced-force philosophy espoused in the document. Instead, the "New Look" doctrine of Eisenhower and his secretary of state, John Foster Dulles, once again placed primary emphasis on nuclear weapons and their delivery by strategic air power. The approach of the new administration in defense matters followed closely the outline of Truman's Air Policy Commission report of 1948. Vigilance and preparedness were the order of the day, largely owing to the pervasive belief that the war in Korea was merely the first of a series of Soviet probes. Arms control was impossible in an atmosphere of war and the threat of a worse war yet to come. In the absence of negotiations or the grounds for some semblance of mutual trust, Washington and Moscow chose the path of arms escalation instead of arms limitation.

7

The Debate Reviewed: Politics or Technology?

The villain of the piece in more than one case has been made weapons technology along with Homo technicus: *the creation of the nuclear mystique, which is rubbing off so disastrously throughout the tiers of the international power structure, was a political act, which technology in its various forms was called in to undo or unmask. The political determinants remain of prime importance.*

— John Erickson, *The Military Technical Revolution*[142]

The decision to launch feasibility studies, eventually culminating in several feasibility tests, did not by itself irrevocably determine the course of the nuclear arms race with the Soviet Union. That course was only begun in earnest, not completely shaped, by the acquisition of the hydrogen bomb. When viewed in the larger context of worsening bilateral relations, the decision to develop the hydrogen bomb was only as inevitable as the mutual failure to develop diplomatic solutions to the most pressing postwar crises.

Although it may be true that American perceptions of a Soviet threat were greatly or even partially exaggerated, those perceptions were nonetheless quite real. In the autumn of 1949, many policymakers in the national security community expected general war to commence within several years. Defense planners based their analyses on adverse Soviet rhetoric and actions. One can only presume that Soviet planners in Moscow reached similar conclusions based on American action.

The Korean War institutionalized the fundamental consensus assumptions held by the foreign policy establishment concerning the bellicose nature of the Soviet state. The notion was prevalent that the Soviet-Chinese-North Korean strike was simply a decoy, initiated to draw U.S. military support from Western Europe (where the real attack would come) to Northeast Asia.

After the war in Korea, the nuclear arms race proceeded along an upward spiral, sustained and reinforced by ingrained distrust, seemingly irreconcilable differences, and imperfect communication. The decision to deploy thermonuclear weapons, once they proved feasible, did not occur in a period of peace. The success of the November 1952 test and the earlier decision of March 1950 to produce hydrogen bombs in quantity, should they prove feasible, assumed heightened relevance because of the deadlocked negotiations to end the Korean conflict. The wartime atmosphere in the United States provided the kind of environment in which nuclear weapons stockpiling could flourish. The Soviet leadership, sensing an increasingly hostile world as well as political capital to be gained by pushing ahead with its program, lagged behind the United States in numbers of weapons but not in their intensity of pursuit.

The January 31 directive was issued in order to begin a technological program for examining the possible military application of fusion. There were no prospects for success in the small amount of work that had been done. There was only the unfounded optimism of Teller, and even he had not seriously committed himself to military fusion research until "after the Russian bomb was dropped."[143] In the words of Han Bethe:

> New calculations were made at Los Alamos, and these new calculations showed that the basis for technical optimism which had existed in the fall of 1949 was very shaky, indeed. The plan which then existed for the making of a hydrogen bomb turned out to be less and less promising as time went on.[144]

Physicists Lawrence, Teller, and Alvarez had briefed AEC and Defense Department officials on several occasions. They never said that the super would be a certain success, although they did, at least once, put the odds at better than one in two. Top government national security officials responsible for budgetary restraint (especially in the austerity-conscious Truman administration) would not ordinarily advance huge sums of money to any project whose certainty was barely 50 percent assured. The urgency instilled in the AEC, State Department, and Defense Department administrators could have come from only one source: their individual and organizational interpretations of growing Soviet power. Teller himself, in the March 1950 issue of the *Bulletin of Atomic Scientists*, asked: "Can a hydrogen bomb be built? How can we build it? Can we build it before the Russians succeed in doing so?"[145] Teller did not have the answers to these questions then, and he certainly did not have the answers in the fall and winter of 1949–1950.

When Oppenheimer testified before the AEC Security Personnel Board in 1954—to clear his name and show that he was not a security risk—his recollections of his role in the hydrogen bomb affair were eagerly sought. He recalled that there were "great technical uncertainties which were both qualitative and quantitative." The chances for success actually declined in the period under consideration (October 5 through January 31); Oppenheimer testified that "the technical prospects for doing what we were planning to do had deteriorated. This was to continue for a long time, and the essential pointers had not yet come up."[146] In his own defense, he told the board:

> I believe that I have never claimed that the hydrogen bomb was not feasible. But I have indicated, starting with early 1950 . . . very strong doubts of the feasibility of anything that was then being worked on. These doubts were right.[147]

The initial stimulus, the Soviet atomic explosion, has been affirmed by all the participants connected with the debate over the hydrogen bor ib. Oppenheimer succinctly summarized the views of Strauss, Teller, Dean, Truman, Acheson, McMahon, and most (if not all) other participants when he said that "no serious controversy arose about the super until the Soviet explosion of an atomic bomb in the autumn of 1949."[148] The Soviet explosion signaled to the world Moscow's determination to be at least the military equal of the United States. The Soviet blast was also a political act in its conception and implementation, aimed at boosting the USSR's status as a world power, consolidating its hold over the satellite states in Eastern Europe, and providing its leadership with the necessary psychological and military tools with which to strengthen its foreign policy.

The Soviet atomic explosion was interpreted in the West as such; they were accused of bellicosity and warposturing. The response of U.S. officialdom was simply that the Russians had caught up, so *we* must move ahead. Prior to the Soviet atomic bomb, the United States survived for four years in the nuclear age without a national debate about building qualitatively different weapons. Only *after* the Soviet Union demonstrated their atomic capability did the policy elite respond.

The members of the Joint Committee on Atomic Energy (except McMahon) were mostly unconcerned with the hydrogen bomb; most, in fact, were not "even conscious that such work was being done."[149] The leadership of the JCAE was very active in searching for new ways to unseat David Lilienthal in his capacity as AEC chairman and in overseeing both the peaceful aspects of atomic energy and the implementation of the fission bomb program. The committee's reactions to the Soviet detonation and the AEC-GAC response was a mixture of rage at and distrust of both the USSR's true motives in setting off an atomic device and the direction in which David Lilienthal and Robert Oppenheimer were supposedly driving the nation's foreign and nuclear policies.

Those who knew most about the physical properties of the atom—the AEC and its scientific advisory body, the GAC—were in an especially uncomfortable position. Their mandate over atomic energy resources extended beyond managerial duties; the AEC was also a decision-making body. The AEC commissioners, however, were tainted (more so than the Defense Department) with the image of running a technical bureaucracy, where politics should be discounted and excluded. Yet the AEC's commissioners were political appointees, not simply university scientists or science administrators. It was inevitable in an area as crucial as atomic energy that political disagreements would arise. These disagreements surfaced most prominently in late 1949 and split the commission, but it is important to note that the arguments put forth in the hydrogen bomb debate were political in every respect. Scientific advice is often not free of political motive. The advice of a scientist in the policy process frequently assumes a political character in that the goal is the persuasion of the president or the Congress; political views often shape or sway the scientist's technical judgment. "While the advice generally appears quite technical, careful analysis of its substance will reveal it to be political in nature."[150]

If we examine, for example, the AEC policy papers and statements concerning the super in the autumn and winter of 1949, we can readily discern a heated political controversy, centering on the implications of the Soviet atomic bomb and the ultimate intentions of the Soviet Union. Once the issue of intentions and consequences was settled, then the proper response to the Soviet nuclear act could be determined. Lilienthal believed the issue went beyond the super; he felt that the development of a new bomb would divert American foreign policy away from negotiations and toward increased hostility with the Soviet Union. Smyth was of the opinion that a decision to proceed with thermonuclear research would ruin the U.S. bid for international nuclear control. Dean and especially Strauss viewed the hypothetical weapon as a sure means of defense against a sworn enemy whose public proclamations and military movements bespoke aggressive intentions.

Finally, it is instructive that the GAC advised on both the technical prospects for the super and the moral and political aspects of the problem. The GAC report of October 30 and the members' individual testimony before the JCAE confirmed the poor technical status of the proposed weapon and their collective belief that, militarily, the super would add only marginally to U.S. defense. Politically, it would negate our oft-repeated statements about U.S. peaceful intentions in the international arena. The GAC's mixture of political and scientific advice is obvious. Regarding the assertion that the GAC members' political views unfairly biased their technological forecast, however, the testimony of Teller, Bradbury, and Alvarez (none of them GAC advisors and two of them hydrogen bomb advocates) verifies the undeveloped and very uncertain status of the hydrogen bomb program before the presidential directive of January 31. The hope of technological breakthrough, then, was subordinated to the grim realities of deterring Stalin's Russia. In the words of Edward Teller, "It just had to be done."[151]

Herbert York writes that "Joe 1," the code name for the first Soviet atomic blast (named for Soviet leader Joseph Stalin), "provided a powerful political stimulus to expand and accelerate the thermonuclear program."[152] The implication given ("expand and accelerate the . . . program") is inaccurate; both Rabi and Teller have noted the lack of any program prior to January 31, 1950. Teller subsequently noted that, although he could not be sure about exact numbers, following the president's directive the number of people working on the super increased to just 10 to 20 percent of the Los Alamos laboratory's efforts. This was still, he said, "a very large increase. As compared to the previous one it was just between standing still and starting to go."[153] The technological impetus from Los Alamos was far outstripped by the political impetus emanating from the "Lawrence-Teller" group.

The idea for a much more powerful weapon, utilizing the lighter elements, had been considered by nuclear physicists since the end of World War II. The Interim Committee of the Manhattan Engineer District, meeting on May 31, 1945, discussed the "stages of development" in bomb categories. Three stages were mentioned, the second of which referred to the booster program and the third to the hydrogen bomb. In the presence of Fermi, Arthur Compton, and Lawrence, Oppenheimer "stated that this was a far more difficult development than the previous stages," but did not discount entirely the possibility of making a super.[154] No dissent was registered from the other scientists present.

The super was then known inside the government as at least a theoretical possibility from at least May 1945, and to many of the administrators involved in the Manhattan Project even earlier. Its development suddenly became an issue in late 1949—not in any of the previous postwar years—because the Soviets made it one by demonstrating their own atomic bomb capability.

At the State and Defense Departments, the bureaucratic machinery was set in motion by Strauss's letter of October 5, 1949. The Policy Planning Staff and the JCS (backed by the Military Liaison Committee) each seized the initiative within their respective organizations. The hydrogen bomb would enhance the influence of both the Policy Planning Staff and the JCS—the former, because of the greater need for long-range, anticipatory forecasting dictated by the new round of events; the latter, because their specialized military advice would remain essential, given the prominence of the military (especially nuclear) dimension of the U.S.-Soviet competition. This is not to imply that the two groups knowingly advocated a course of action they thought would lead to an unpredictable arms race; the Policy Planning Staff under Kennan opposed the super. Rather, organizational concerns at the time the decision was made (that is, when Nitze ran the Policy Planning Staff) coincided (or were equated with) perceived strategic need.

The Policy Planning Staff, though, was merely one small (yet highly influential) part of the State Department. A good case can be made that the State Department would have better fulfilled its bureaucratic mandate had it followed Kennan's rather than Nitze's advice. The struggle for international control of nuclear weaponry (that is, the fight to elevate international control to the top of the foreign policy agenda) was effectively ended once the decision to proceed with feasibility testing was made. The State Department's role in setting Truman's strategic direction was thereafter subordinated to other agencies within the national security bureaucracy, because the paradigm demanding negotiations was rejected while the paradigm demanding weapons stockpiling was favored. Doctrinal justification for such a strategy further demanded a leading role for the Department of Defense.

Truman's respect for Acheson's opinion was still very strong, however, during the hydrogen bomb debate. Warner Schilling has written that the State Department was the most important organization in this decision; he concludes from extensive interviewing and research:

> The State Department representatives reflected a concern for the diplomatic opportunities the Russians would gain from such a monopoly for political blackmail around the Soviet periphery.[155]

Acheson shared this concern and so ignored Kennan's advice in recommending for development. The American people, he said, "would not tolerate a policy of delaying nuclear research while we sought for further ways of reaching accommodation with the Russians."[156] The central theme emerging from the arguments of Acheson and Johnson was the necessity to prepare for Soviet military action. They had to make a political decision based on unfavorable technological data. Their stated motive for endorsing the hydrogen bomb was that, in an uncertain world facing a hostile, nuclear-armed adversary, risk taking had to be minimized. The Soviet Union might already have been at work on the hydrogen bomb; therefore, the United States could not afford to presume that Russian intentions were peaceful. The notion of the hydrogen bomb as a deterring (and a superior war-fighting) vehicle was being promulgated. In the tradition of Clausewitz, Acheson believed that if the hydrogen bomb added to strategic deterrence, the weapon would be merely a special tool with which to further U.S. political ends.

Finally, President Truman's predisposition in the decision stemmed from his deeply held conviction that the Soviet Union held aggressive intentions in regard to Western Europe and the United States. There are differing accounts of Truman's motives and actions during the fall and winter of 1949–1950. In his memoirs, Truman states that although the Soviet detonation of late August 1949 "came sooner than the experts had estimated . . . it did not require us to alter the direction of our program."[157]

Since the Soviet atomic bomb directly affected the U.S. military atomic energy program, ultimately causing a sizable shift from fission to fusion warheads, this statement must be regarded as misleading. Not sure himself what the chances for technological success would be, Truman believed that it was imperative for the U.S. armed forces to be preeminent—as the only sure guarantor of peace. If the weapon proved feasible, then Truman could not afford *not* to stockpile it—both at home and abroad. His January 31 decision simply called for feasibility studies (not directly for a feasibility test); this was the easiest decision politically, since it superficially changed very little.[158] In actuality, however, Truman's directive began the technological quest in earnest, eventually achieving the objective set on March 10, 1950—the successful feasibility test of November 1952.

In another version of events, Truman approved the program the previous fall, when the AEC's budget was being decided. Funds were earmarked for a concerted weapons-enhancement program, not because Truman knew or even thought that the hydrogen bomb was a scientific certainty but because he thought that a decision to proceed with research in this direction (that is, toward bigger and more powerful weaponry) would further the nation's stated policy goal of reaching an accommodation with the USSR. His assistant press secretary, Eben Ayers, recorded the following entry in his diary on February 4, 1950—five days after the presidential decision:

> At one of our staff sessions this week there was some discussion of the stories and talk about the hydogen bomb. . . . The President said there actually was no decision to make on the H-bomb. He said this really was a question that was settled in making up the budget for the Atomic Energy Commission last fall when $300,000,000 was allotted. He said he had discussed that last September with David Lilienthal, Chairman of the atomic energy commission, Secretary of State Acheson, and Secretary of Defense Johnson. He went on to say that we had got to do it—make the bomb—though no one wants to use it. But, he said, we have got to have it if only for bargaining purposes with the Russians.[159]

If this was true, then the decision to proceed with the H-bomb was settled before the Strauss letter of October 5 was written. The months of interagency debate were unimportant because the decision had already been made—though, in one sense, the positive recommendation given by the special committee of the NSC in January 1950 would have confirmed the president's budgetary decision.

The *Seventh Semiannual Report* of the AEC, published in January 1950, acknowledged that in "early October [1949] the President released budgetary reserves so as to advance by some months the *start of a quarter-billion dollar expansion program*, then at the drawing-board stage and planned for construction in subsequent fiscal years."[160] The president allotted $358 million for operations and $340 million for plant and equipment for FY 1951.[161] The estimated cost of the hydrogen bomb development program was $300 million, according to Ayers's diary, Truman's *Memoirs*, and the March 9 special committee report—to be spread over several years (estimated to run from calendar year 1950 to 1953). The increase in the AEC budget from FY 1949 to FY 1950 was $67 million—$65 million for operations, and only $2 million for plant and equipment. If we make allowances for heavier funding levels toward the end of the three-year development span, then the "quarter-billion dollar expansion program" may have been an oblique reference to the new thermonuclear program. The heavy emphasis on operations, though, as opposed to expansion of existing plant and equipment in FY 1950, would probably not have provided the Los Alamos laboratory with the necessary funding needed to begin a concentrated effort on the super.

The "early October" release of budgetary reserves may or may not have been the final word on the subject. Funds could have been approved for a thermonuclear project and very easily diverted to the regular fission program without much loss if the NSC special committee had persuaded Truman to decide against the super on January 31, 1950. The March 9 special committee report stated:

> If the hydrogen ignition should prove infeasible, most of the expenditure toward production preparations would not be lost since the production capacity would be employed for fission weapons, radiological warfare agents, or other purposes.[162]

Still, there is good reason to believe that the decision was not decided in the manner and at the time recorded in Ayers's diary; none of the other participants in the decision referred to it all (that is, the October 1949 AEC budgetary decision as the final word), and the accounts and observations of the three principals mentioned—Lilienthal, Acheson, and Johnson—do not mesh with Ayers's observation.

The particular historiography, however, does not alter the evidence that the determinative forces motivating Truman and his closest advisors were political in nature. He wanted the hydrogen bomb "for bargaining purposes with the Russians," to induce Stalin and the Soviet leadership to reach a mutually beneficial settlement on the remaining outstanding issues in Soviet-American relations. In this respect, Truman's view of the potentialities of the hydrogen bomb were similar to his 1945 concept (and that of former Secretary of State James Byrnes) of the diplomatic value of the atomic bomb. Truman perceived advantages (for example, at the postwar conference table) in the possession of demonstrably powerful nuclear weapons. The policy of using nuclear weapons to strengthen the U.S. bargaining position with the Soviet Union did not work in 1945–1946, and it failed in 1950 (and subsequently) as well.

The hydrogen bomb decision was made in an environment of Soviet-American hostility during the formation of the early Cold War arms race. The highest echelon of U.S. government advisors was faced with a political reality (the Soviet Union as an adversary and its sudden, unexpected possession of an atomic bomb), and they were asked to make a political recommendation. The alternatives were discussed, analyzed, and then discarded, one by one, until the final choice in favor of development was made. Although the composition of the administration and the Congress in 1949 tended to structure the decision in a politically biased way (toward development), the policy papers were written, the different viewpoints debated, and the decision taken—despite technological uncertainty in all quarters.

The determinants of the Soviet-American arms race, then, must be conceived of as political in nature. These political determinants derived from conscious and well-ordered (not necessarily correct) notions concerning the international state system and the appropriate place of each great power in that system. A rivalry as great as the nuclear arms race may well be fed by technological advances, but its inspiration can only be drawn from the failures inherent in political vision. With two world views as distinct and inharmonious as the American and the Soviet, with two states possessing opposing global interests and values, and with two states (and only two) as militarily powerful as the American and the Soviet, it is not surprising that the Grand Alliance of World War II should have given way to the nuclear antagonism of postwar years.

8 The Politics of Strategic Defense

We are not engaged in an arms race, but rather in a race of technology. The former emphasizes the quantity of arms, the latter their quality and particularly the element of novelty. —Edward Teller[163]

The hydrogen bomb decision is not an isolated example of the primacy of political developments and political forces over technological pull in the postwar Soviet-American arms race—or in any of the major pre–World War II arms races. In answering the question of what set of factors prompts a state to innovate in the first instance, the historical record provides a great deal of insight into the forces that drive technological innovation.

Thus, in the period between 1870 and 1914, a variety of economic stresses and strains (including industrialization, urbanization, and a population increase of 10 percent per decade)[164] aggravated European social conditions that, in turn, directly affected each nation's foreign policy. Long-standing mutual fears, greatly exaggerated by jingoistic politicians, found expression in large part through naval and land-based armaments competition (between Germany and England, England and France, France/Russia and Germany, Japan and Russia), which was well received by leading opinion makers of the day.

One symptom of the European powers' drive to win local prestige and greater extraregional influence was the aforementioned multilateral arms race. When the French and Russian fleets surpassed the Royal Navy numerically in 1899, Britain embarked on a massive naval building program that "intensified the naval race."[165] Britain's alarm at the steady growth in Franco-Russian naval strength was shared by the German monarchy, itself anxious over Parliament's reaction as well as the menacing Franco-Russian entente. In a relatively few years, the German Empire's military and industrial potential equaled that of its European rivals.

The naval arms race before 1914 bears at least one major similarity to the post-1945 arms race. Both can be characterized as multilateral competitions, though only two states stand out: imperial Germany was building against the Triple Entente but had Britain primarily in mind, while Britain concentrated on Germany after it had entered the race; whereas today, the USSR arms itself against a perceived coalition of enemies, but the principal nuclear opponent remains the United States. In each arms race, then, two adversaries have predominated in the context of a larger multilateral contest.

51

After World War II—and the construction of the atomic and hydrogen bombs—full-scale military rocket procurement and deployment (in the form of long-range intermediate and, later, intercontinental missilery) received a tremendous boost from the intelligence gathered concerning early Soviet interest in rocketry. A review of strategic programs was initiated very early in the Eisenhower administration, prodded by frequent U.S. intelligence estimates of Soviet missile progress. Subsequently, in 1954, the Strategic Missile Evaluation Committee concluded that long-range missile technology could be developed. The next year, the NSC "officially assigned top national priority" to the liquid-fueled Air Force Atlas ICBM project.[166] In short, "US missile development efforts from 1954 through the middle of 1957 were largely motivated by the desire to prevent the USSR from acquiring a lead in the strategic missile field."[167]

Progress in the technological arms race must be planned years in advance, and, because of the always uncertain nature of technological innovation, one can never be certain that a proposed system will work as envisaged.[168] It is manifest that, in an arms race, the technological planning for new systems—once a program has been ordered—almost always arises from the perception that staying abreast or ahead is essential for national security. Scientific ideas usually defy rational planning. In the Soviet-American arms race, however, scientific *innovation* has occurred more at the behest of political stimuli than because of the lure (or creep) of technology.

The hydrogen bomb was the precursor of the advanced technology arms race. It was and is the most powerful explosive fashioned by man, and all the subsequent changes in the past thirty years have taken the form of delivery vehicles for or modifications in the nuclear warhead's use.[169] In fact, the trend has been to develop weapons systems of smaller dimensions and greater discrimination, in large part because politicians and strategists want choices and increased flexibility of response. In essence, the early arms race received a powerful stimulus in the winter and spring of 1949–1950, when President Truman decided to attempt the development of the super and to forge ahead with its mass production should it prove feasible.

In an atmosphere of intense hostility during the Korean War—believed by many in 1950 to have been planned in Moscow—the hydrogen bomb's development in 1952 did not lead to the anticipated bargaining chip but instead reinforced the Soviet hydrogen bomb program and so contributed to the institutionalization of the nuclear arms race. Negotiations on limiting new systems were not possible because of the worsening political climate—at the one time when such nascent weapons might have been stopped. Although some progress was made thereafter (for example, the 1963 Limited Test Ban Treaty), twenty years passed before President Nixon and General-Secretary

Brezhnev agreed to begin placing limits on nuclear delivery vehicles in the first Strategic Arms Limitation Agreement of 1972.

SALT I was accompanied by an equally important document: the Anti-Ballistic Missile Treaty. One of the enduring truisms of the arms race was ratified in that accord—the superiority of offensive over defensive systems. The acquisition of the hydrogen bomb, the development of accurate intercontinental ballistic missiles (ICBMs), and the fractionation of missile warheads (multiple independently targetable reentry vehicles, or MIRVs) provide an attacker (or "arms depriver") with a far greater capability to destroy selected targets than an opponent has to defend them. The incalculable destructive effects of numerous nuclear weapons detonations against undefended population and industrial centers, coupled with the certainty that a significant percentage of strategic nuclear forces will survive a first strike and be able to retaliate in kind, form the basis of "mutual assured destruction" (MAD).

Deterrence has rested upon MAD since the mid-1950s, when the Soviet Union began accumulating a nuclear weapons stockpile of its own to challenge U.S. nuclear leadership. As offensive weapons stockpiling increased in the absence of any credible defensive doctrine or countervailing weapons, the arms race acquired MAD as the only plausible management vehicle available. MAD best described the evolving hostage relationship unfolding between the superpowers and thus gave rise to specific deterrent policies that, in turn, reinforced MAD. As with Winston Churchill's remark that democracy is the worst form of government except for every other form of government, so the adherents of deterrence believed that only assured destruction (however uncomfortable the reality) could keep the peace.

Successive administrations considered and susequently rejected civil or strategic defense. Secretary of Defense Robert McNamara did not approve Project Defender, civil defense funding was tightly constrained in the Kennedy and Johnson administrations, and in 1969 the Senate voted by a margin of one to build an extensive antiballistic missile (ABM) network to defend cities and ICBM silos. Throughout the ABM debate, many analysts argued (in support of the ABM) that the requisite technology was either at hand or could be developed in due course and that defensive protection was a wiser and more politically acceptable course than threatening universal destruction.

Opponents of the ABM countered that the foreseeable technology marshaled for defense could always be overwhelmed at far less cost and that a doctrinal shift from deterrence to defense was inherently unstable because it would create the impression that the United States was preparing a preemptive strike. Effective defenses, it was argued, would enable the United States to strike with impunity, because the USSR would not then have been capable of mounting more than a nominal counterattack. Deterrence would thus be undermined and crisis stability diminished. The implications of the 1969 deterrence versus defense debate, now being fought anew with the decision to pursue a multilayered strategic defense system, will be discussed at greater length in the next chapter.

When the United States and the Soviet Union agreed to restrict "development, testing, and deployment" of ABM systems in 1972, deterrence premised on MAD was temporarily salvaged—temporarily because the concept of active strategic defense is perceived by many to be a more worthy goal than the preservation of a deterrence system based on a complex web of rationality and uncertainty. Proponents of strategic defense frequently offer moral arguments on behalf of their strategy ("It is immoral to threaten mass destruction but perfectly moral to attempt self-defense"), and for this reason alone defensive strategies will periodically emerge as an alternative to MAD. Technological improvements and advances will also be cited as an important reason to pursue a defensive strategy. As in the hydrogen bomb decision, however, it is my contention that a constellation of political forces convinced President Reagan early in 1983 to begin the quest for a space-based defense. Technology (and especially the promise of new, uncertain approaches) was used by key proponents as a means to achieve a political goal: the elimination of MAD through the substitution of active defense. Further, there is good reason to believe that even when the applicability of emerging technologies was introduced into the decision-making process, the adherents of strategic defense—including the president himself—fully appreciated the immature state of the proposed weapons systems.

Research on ballistic missile defense (BMD) continued to be funded (at very low levels) in the United States after the 1972 ABM treaty, primarily on the grounds that it would be imprudent not to investigate BMD concepts that the USSR (with bigger research budgets) might be pursuing. The fear of a "technology surprise" and a rapid Soviet "break-out" from the ABM treaty kept limited BMD funding alive throughout the 1970s. Flirtation with directed-energy weapons (in government laboratories, in the defense industry, and in universities) became more respectable as advances in associated technologies (for example, fiber optics for rapid communication) made lasers and particle beams more thinkable and perhaps less expensive.

Improvements in technology relevant to BMD did not, however, advance far enough to convince the policy community that defensive weapons systems were worthy of a second look. In 1980, President Carter's final year in office, Michael Deane noted that although "some exploratory research is being conducted" under the auspices of the Department of Defense, "no real optimism exists for the possibility of creating an effective weapon.[170] Similarly, in assessing the new technologies as recently as 1981, William

Kincade wondered whether directed-energy weapons "will pass the test of engineering feasibility." Space-based defense was considered only for "the more distant future," and only then because new fears concerning hostile Soviet space activities above and beyond antisatellite weapons (ASATs) rekindled U.S. interest in pursuing additional BMD research.[171]

Finally, Edward Teller—long a proponent of building active defenses—wrote in 1980:

> There are claims that particle beams are effective over vast distances, but such claims seem premature. There is real hope, however, that particle beams could aid in defense against incoming missiles that are as close as a few miles.[172]

Teller was more optimistic about lasers but offered no timeframe for their introduction into future arsenals. Teller's laser optimism derives, in part, from his attachment to defense over deterrence, having recently declared the physics of laser weapons sound. Many physicists and engineers, however, challenge the fundamental premises of all directed-energy weapons designated to disable or destroy missiles and reentry vehicles. Although politics abounds on both sides of the BMD debate, it remains necessary for space defense enthusiasts to defend the theoretical and technological feasibility of their designs, regardless of the motivation of skeptics.

Such skepticism is not only found in the university community, often the major source of disagreement. In early 1982, the comptroller general of the United States reported:

> Significant technical uncertainties remain to be resolved before even a limited first-generation weapon system is possible. The uncertainties relate to all aspects of the system.[173]

The uncertainties in "all aspects of the system" refer to the Defense Advanced Research Projects Agency (DARPA) space-triad program, in which preliminary laser development, large optics, and acquisition/tracking/precision pointing research was and still is being conducted under the respective names Alpha, LODE (large optics demonstration experiment), and Talon Gold.

The Pentagon, in fact, began to review all facets of its space policy in August 1981, primarily because officials in the new Reagan administration expressed a greater desire to exploit military prospects in space than did their predecessors under President Carter. The review was completed one year later and remains classified, but a fact sheet issued at that time declared that there were no "new directions in space weaponry," and, apart from greater organizational integration of research (then fragmented in each of the separate services), Defense Department space policy remained virtually unchanged[174]—despite the creation of a space command under Air Force auspices.

In September 1982, shortly after the announcement of the Defense Department's space policy and President Reagan's July 4 speech on moving forward in space exploration and development, Richard DeLauer (the under secretary of defense for research and engineering) testified before the Senate Foreign Relations Subcommittee on Arms Control that space weapons development might be possible, but "probably not in the near future."[175] The military posture report of the JCS for FY 1983 mentions a "vigorous" endoatmospheric defense program only, except to note that work continues in the "advancement of the BMD technology base to support future system concepts."[176] Both DeLauer and the JCS believed in 1982 that space-based defense was at best a very long-term proposition, one that present technologies or "system concepts" could not support.

On February 1, 1983, Secretary of Defense Caspar Weinberger's annual report to Congress was released, in which the principal space focus was placed upon ASATs. Directed-energy systems were seen as strengthening the U.S. ASAT program (which is being designed to deter Soviet ASAT use by threatening Moscow's communications and surveillance satellites) and as providing a necessary hedge against Soviet ABM breakout:

> To support an anti-satellite capability beyond this decade, we are currently assessing the feasibility of space-based laser weapons.
>
> The program is structured, therefore, to sustain our understanding of this technology so that we could field an advanced and highly effective BMD system quickly should the need arise.[177]

Feasibility assessment (primarily of lasers) was planned to more than treble from actual expenditures of $462.1 million in FY 1982 to a proposed authorization of $1.5 billion in FY 1985. Momentum for a serious and sustained BMD program, initially linked to ASAT development, had built to the point where ample research and development funding would be allocated. BMD research was clearly seen as an important adjunct to ASAT development, in which new applications that would take many years to produce in the form of full-fledged space defenses could be spun off earlier to attain less grandiose but more achievable ASAT systems.

As the references cited earlier indicate, the technology of space-based defense was quite uncertain by early 1983, with many outstanding scientific issues escaping resolution. Teller had periodically urged the president to begin an active strategic defense program, in large part to resolve many of the problems encountered by those theorizing about or experimenting with small-scale lasers. In early February 1983, at a meeting with the secretary of defense and the JCS, President Reagan reportedly favored beginning a technology development program to assess feasibility. The president was concerned about reports of Soviet ASAT and BMD progress and about more immediate political difficulties regarding congressional opposition to MX ICBM production and deployment and more general discontent, as measured by the strength of the nuclear freeze movement.[a] The most important factor, however, as indicated in his March 23 "Star Wars" speech, was the president's desire to shift doctrinal emphasis over the long term from the strategy of deterrence to a strategy of defense.

Teller was not alone in urging such a doctrinal shift; among the many organizations and individuals who pressed for strategic defense, perhaps the most prominent and most relentless was retired Air Force General Daniel O. Graham. General Graham's Project High Frontier, conducted under the auspices of the Heritage Foundation, stimulated and focused much of the renewed public debate on BMD. It must be discussed before further examination and analysis of President Reagan's controversial "Star Wars" speech of March 23, 1983.

High Frontier is not a concatenation of exotic technologies, nor is it primarily a technology development program. It is a strategy—"a new national strategy," as the subtitle of General Graham's book would have it. The goal is simply to replace MAD with a new doctrine of assured survival, thereby nullifying the Soviet military threat. Additional benefits would accrue over time as the industrialization of space follows the construction of exoatmospheric defenses.[178]

The Graham proposal holds that weapons systems available today permit the United States to achieve a "technological end-run on the Soviets." High Frontier posits a layered or multitiered defense consisting of two levels of space-based platforms and a ground-based point (or terminal) defense network, supplemented by passive civil defense measures. The first tier would be designed to intercept Soviet ICBMs in the boost phase, or roughly within the first four to five minutes of flight. "Boost-phase intercept," as it has come to be known, is the most critical element in BMD operations, both because the missile initially travels at slower speeds (and is therefore easier to disable or destroy) and, more important, because the MIRVed launcher at this stage of its trajectory has not yet launched its separately targetable reentry vehicles. A kill in the boost phase, therefore, greatly reduces the number of targets to be tracked and intercepted by the remaining defensive layers. To illustrate the critical nature of boost phase intercept, it should be recalled that one Soviet SS-18 "bus" can as a practical matter deliver fourteen reentry vehicles (without SALT II limitations).

---

[a]In August 1982, the congressional freeze resolution failed in the House of Representatives by two votes.

The second tier is projected as a broader space-based network, perhaps utilizing, in the future, "advanced beam weaponry." The second tier would intercept deployed reentry vehicles in the postboost phase (and during mid-course flight)—that is, those warheads launched from Soviet ICBMs that survive the boost-phase interception. The final active defense system based on earth to defend U.S. missile fields and launch control centers would finally attempt to destroy any remaining reentry vehicles. The entire apparatus is called Global Ballistic Missile Defense (GBMD), implying a capability to defend allies as well as the continental United States. General Graham claims that an effective GBMD could be deployed by 1987–1988, "given adequate priority."[179]

High Frontier differs from its space-based competitors in that its sponsors suggest the possibility of near-term deployment using "off-the-shelf," conventional weapons technologies. The entire gamut of requirements necessary to fully implement General Graham's vision—improved space transportation, a manned low-earth orbit space station, high-capacity energy systems, and commercial exploitation—are claimed to be with us today. The technology is here or readily within grasp: High Frontier does not "demand technological 'breakthroughs' or a commitment to mere scientific theories."[180] The program can achieve all its objectives for approximately $40 billion in constant dollars through 1990; greater savings are factored in through eliminating the need for costly new weapons of deterrence (for example, MX).

Graham's influence on Pentagon planners and other national security officials remained largely confined to program managers directing the various BMD component projects and certain space mission officers. Politically conservative groups, senators, and government appointees, however, seized upon the idea (if not always its specifics) as a means to reestablish military superiority. Senator Malcolm Wallop (Republican of Wyoming) began lobbying for laser battle stations in 1979, similarly claiming that the technology was at hand for minimal cost. The issue, especially since 1981 (when Senator Wallop convinced a number of his conservative Republican colleagues to support increased laser defense funding),[181] has divided along ideological lines: conservatives generally favor a strategic shift toward space defense, whereas liberals oppose deviation from MAD.

The technology of High Frontier found a less receptive audience. Few people in the bureaucracy at any level believed in the near-term credibility of the Graham concept, based as it is on a relatively simple network of satellites and nonnuclear projectiles. More than 400 orbiting satellites armed with 20,000 conventionally armed "kill vehicles" would be positioned in the next few years to destroy Soviet ICBMs during their boost phase. As a result, there was initially pervasive skepticism.

Despite numerous briefings given by General Graham and his staff in both the executive and the legislative branches, serious questions of systems viability could not be answered satisfactorily. The president's decision to proceed with space-based defense reflects this skepticism, as the program envisaged will not comprise High Frontier's off-the-shelf hardware. George Keyworth, the president's science advisor and director of the Office of Science and Technology Policy—and an important voice arguing for defense over deterrence—said in 1982 that he had "many, many technological concerns about the validity of the particular proposals."[182]

Air Force Lt. Colonel Donald S. Harlacher has characterized High Frontier as a strategy based on illusion. There are operational constraints, for example, on both long-wavelength infrared and short-wavelength infrared sensors used in acquiring and tracking ICBM signatures. As the missile moves into its postboost (and especially reentry) phase, "it is questionable . . . if a shortwave infrared sensor could detect and track the progressively smaller and colder targets."[183] Short-wavelength sensors, as featured in High Frontier (and slated to receive much of the new R&D tracking emphasis) are better suited to boost-phase intercepts. The reliability of a layered defense, however, requires not simply redundancy but a much stronger reserve backstop if even a small percentage of Soviet ICBMs should penetrate the first layer and deploy their numerous reentry vehicles. Present sensor technologies are far from sufficient to perform the required tasks.

High Frontier estimates that kill vehicle velocity should be about 3,000 feet per second, whereas the necessary velocities, given Graham's constraints, would need to be "at least several times that estimated." Achieving these higher velocities implies "substantial trade-offs in both cost and weight." Additionally, the command, control, and communications (C^3) functions become critical as extremely complex discrimination and sorting problems (for example, which reentry vehicles are real and which are decoys?) are coupled with very short reaction and intercept times. The C^3 system, in short, "must be far more sophisticated than anything heretofore encountered."[184]

Two further problems, though there are others, concern the GBMD's lack of a self-generating refire capability and the vulnerability of ground-based point defense to nuclear attack and electromagnetic pulse.[185] In fact, the entire network would be riddled with technical constraints and uncertainties and would be exceedingly vulnerable to relatively simple and inexpensive countermeasures. Because of the short time frame, the high degree of systems integration and interdependence between the C^3 and intercept functions in space and on earth, and the requirement that near-perfect component efficiencies will be essential, High Frontier's contribution to the decision-making process was limited to its doctrinal stimulus, rather than its notion of a quick and painless technological fix.

The specifics of High Frontier failed to convince Teller, Keyworth, DeLauer, or the JCS, but the strategy it espoused struck a responsive chord in an administration that was wary of the "arms control syndrome." Simply put, the professional arms control community was and is seen as slavishly devoted to the *process* of (incremental) negotiation rather than to the achievement of concrete results in the national interest. Arms control is perceived to be detrimental because it serves to tranquilize the American public (as in SALT I and II) while permitting selective Soviet advantages (necessary to keep the process alive).

In this context, such advocates of strategic defense as Teller and Weinberger believed that attempting to negotiate military restraint in space was futile and would only strengthen the Soviet lead in space-based BMD. Negotiations either would be endless and inconclusive or would prove disadvantageous to the U.S. military space program, while Soviet R&D continued unabated.[186]

Setting in train a concerted technology development program, then, was decidedly preferable to pursuing the perceived chimera of a mutually balanced space agreement with Moscow. The president and his advisors, interested in superiority through defensive invulnerability, would not be deflected from their objective of altering the current strategic balance by the arms control lobby's purported zeal to negotiate under any set of conditions.

Therefore, on March 23, 1983, President Reagan announced that the United States would be better served by a strategy of defense through BMD than by the riskier strategy of deterrence. The president made plain the challenges and difficulties inherent in his plan: "I know this is a formidable technical task, one that may not be accomplished before the end of the century."[187] The speech quickly became known as the "Star Wars" speech, as it seemed to call upon scientists to base exotic weapons in space—and so was widely interpreted as a call to carry the arms race into the heretofore restricted sanctuary beyond the earth's atmosphere.

The president issued a National Security Decision Directive (NSDD) on March 25 to "direct the development of an intensive effort *to define* a long-term research and development program" (emphasis added) to remove the nuclear ballistic missile threat. The president's press release of March 25 also stated:

> In order to provide the necessary basis for this effort, I further direct a study be completed on a priority basis to assess the roles that ballistic missile defense could play in future security strategy of the United States and our allies. Among other items, the study will provide guidance necessary to develop research and development funding commitments for the FY 1985 Departmental budgets and the accompanying Five-Year Defense Program (FYDP).[188]

Prior to the Reagan speech, Thomas C. Cooper, assistant secretary of the Air Force for research, development, and logistics, testified before

Congress that although the charged particle beam—one of the two likeliest candidates (along with lasers) to be funded for advanced BMD experimentation—held the best "military potential . . . [it was] way out there."[189] Several days after the speech, then-Deputy Secretary of Defense Paul Thayer said in reference to the decision: "This truly is a vision, and that's about all it is at this stage of the game."[190]

In April 1983, the President's Commission on Strategic Forces (the Scowcroft Commission) issued its recommendation on MX basing and the future of the U.S. ICBM program. The report's findings on BMD were especially relevant, given the close timing of the star wars speech and the release of the Scowcroft report. While citing "vigorous" Soviet R&D programs, the report concluded that "applications of current technology offer no real promise of being able to defend the United States against massive nuclear attack in this century."[191] The close interaction between the work of the Scowcroft Commission and top national security officials strongly suggests that the administration was well apprised of the technological uncertainty surrounding space-based BMD. The president endorsed the panel's report in full. Similarly, retired Air Force General Bernard Schriever, who was responsible for supervising much of the early U.S. missile program, said that "there are a lot of challenges, probably more than when we started our development of the ICBM."[192]

The March 25 NSDD set in motion two study panels, one to assess the technological parameters and the other to address international implications and treaty obligations. The two reports were written between June 1 and October 1, 1983, and remain classified. The latter study, directed by Fred Hoffman of the defense consulting firm Pan Heuristics, is known as the Future Security Strategy Study. It reportedly did not conclude that accelerated research into advanced BMD necessarily violates the 1972 ABM Treaty, nor did the study project adverse allied reaction. Should an extensive, layered BMD prove feasible and desirable, the ABM Treaty would only then have to be abrogated. According to the study, a defensive shield would create further uncertainty in the minds of Soviet planners and would therefore add to deterrence.

Although the studies are classified, the magazine *Aviation Week and Space Technology* obtained copies and quoted freely in a four-part BMD series between October and December 1983. The focus of attention was the technology report issued by the Defensive Technologies Study Team, directed by former NASA Administrator James Fletcher. The study, known as the Fletcher Report, is simultaneously optimistic and cautious; a careful analysis of the leaked report's contents is required because of *Aviation Week*'s particularly sanguine and selective interpretation of the technologies and scientific principles in question.

The first installment of articles began with the report's recommendation: "With vigorous technology development programs, the potential for ballistic missile defense can be demonstrated by the early 1990s." Three principal avenues in laser research are recommended, as are particle beams and nonnuclear projectiles (using a hypervelocity electromagnetic railgun). The laser program looks toward the rapid development of infrared chemical lasers, ground-based excimer lasers, and short-wavelength chemical lasers. A number of feasibility tests are called for between 1985 and 1988; costs could total $27 billion through FY 1989 and (for a deployed, layered system) about $95 billion through 2000.[193]

The report admits that BMD in space is not yet credible and cautions against a crash program, stating that a rapid technology demonstration and a rushed deployment "of marginal or brittle systems based on available technology" is inadvisable.[194] The Fletcher conferees thus distanced themselves from the principal High Frontier theme that a *feasible* BMD network could be deployed in several years with existing technologies, and they also opened the study to charges from critics (such as General Graham and Senator Wallop) that the study was characteristic of the "R&D forever crowd" allegedly dominating the Pentagon research establishment.

Two additional ideas were introduced as potential weapons components in the panel's report. Antimatter particle beams as a possible kill mechanism and the use of "extraterrestrial resources to provide large amounts of mass in Earth orbit for . . . shields and high inertia platforms" were suggested as realistic candidates. Beam weapons would probably demand energy output greater than 100 MeV (million electron volts) to intercept ballistic missiles. "Such energies require very large space-based accelerators and multimegawatt power sources."

Antimatter beams, however, are claimed to be practicable with accelerators generating energies at just 4 to 20 MeV. As *Aviation Week* acknowledges, though, questions remain in the production and storage of "sufficient quantities" of antimatter[195]—hardly incidental issues. Energy production and storage (even at the reduced energies needed for the anti-matter approach) are two central, but by no means the only, bottlenecks in beam propagation and in fact present formidable obstacles that are only hinted at in the magazine's zeal to promote defense in space.

The second installment expanded upon the introductory article. *Aviation Week* reported that the technologies most desired were often the least advanced, and that there would be correspondingly "major technical uncertainties." The report argued, however, that although a system designed to be 99.9 percent effective is not "technically credible," an imperfect BMD system would be preferable to none at all, because it would wean Moscow away from offensive weapons deployment toward a similar defensive strategy.[196]

The report is also cited as stating that much of the high-altitude technology needed to discriminate between real targets, on the one hand, and penetration aids and decoys, on the other, is either available today or expected in the near future, and it is similarly optimistic about progress in exo-atmospheric interceptor systems. The space shuttle, however, must first be able to launch loads of 100 tons or more to medium orbits many times each year.[197] As the present shuttle's rated load capacity is roughly 32 tons, heavy-lift launch vehicles must first be developed that are capable of carrying more than three times NASA's shuttle capacity well beyond low-earth orbit.

No task appears too daunting for the editors of *Aviation Week;* readers are blithely told that technological problems include system survivability against nuclear blast or laser attack, affordable nonnuclear interceptors, and the "tools for developing battle management software"—as if, to use Teller's phrase upon hearing the wording of Truman's hydrogen bomb decision, a system could be produced "by tightening a few last screws."

The impression is consistently maintained that the solution to complex (and as yet poorly understood) technological problems is either at hand or capable of early resolution. The report is said, for example, to have set out the need to establish technology by 1986 to permit the proper scaling required for beam generators, neutral particle beams, excimer, free electron, X-ray lasers, and infrared chemical lasers.[198]

At the same time, the report concluded that present technology will not be sufficient to meet a variety of emerging Soviet threats.[199] The article did not, however, offer any operational guidance pertaining to the particle beam generator's performance level, nor was there a definition of the "scaling" that will be needed. For reasons that will be discussed later, it is highly unlikely that a prototype system can be properly scaled up and tested for many years—certainly not by 1986. The NATO Assembly's scientific and technical report on space-based BMD (prompted by President Reagan's March speech) contended that the "practical obstacles to be overcome are daunting," extending to the development of new energy-generating devices and the need for "phenomenal accuracy."[200]

The third article in *Aviation Week's* BMD series focused on two themes: the use of the space shuttle to demonstrate high-energy laser and kinetic energy "hit-to-kill" weapons and an elaboration of the proposed directed-energy concepts. Teledyne Brown Engineering has proposed a two-year, three-phase "Validator" program that relies on the shuttle for early space testing of "existing technologies and off-the-shelf hardware"[201]—reminiscent of similar High Frontier claims. Teledyne Brown's program would demonstrate either lasers or kinetic energy weapons. The set of chemical laser concepts, one of several options deemed worthy of further purusal by the Fletcher Panel, was reported by a White House office to be "idled" in favor of accelerating short-wavelength technologies.[202] The mid-infrared chemical lasers are among the most mature laser technologies experimented with today, however, and even here the report states scale-up will require an additional six to eight orders of magnitude to obtain a successful system.[203] Obtaining militarily-relevant results with the shorter-wavelength approach (critical for the boost-phase intercept plan) will consume much additional time, as the technology is in its infant stages.

Neutral (rather than charged) particle beams are considered to hold great potential, but *Aviation Week* reports that the Fletcher group advised that the physics of neutral particle beams be further explored on a more basic level before experimenting with high-energy beam weapons. The magazine adds that beam spreading will be a problem unless new technologies are developed to cope with such dispersion.[204] These are longer-range problems that must eventually be resolved, but all the Fletcher recommendations will first require tremendous scaling to very high energy levels. The projected scaling alone of the major directed-energy and ultra-high-speed kinetic energy systems under consideration range from an increase of seven to eighteen orders of magnitude greater than at present. The Fletcher Report itself says that achieving scaling of five orders of magnitude for one of the laser requirements will consume about ten years' time.[205] Colin Gray, a prominent advocate of ASAT development and strategic defense, acknowledges that both scientific and engineering obstacles remain: we do not yet "know how to design, construct, and loft into orbit a particle beam accelerator that could function as a practical weapon." The accelerator must be greatly scaled down in size and weight, while the energy output needed to perform standard space-based BMD missions must be vastly scaled up simultaneously.[206]

The final set of paired articles in *Aviation Week*'s BMD series, which appeared in early December 1983, discussed the importance of boost-phase intercept and hypervelocity technology. The time range given by the Fletcher Report for boost-phase intercepts is extremely limited—150 to 300 seconds—particularly upon consideration that 2,000 boosters must be targeted.[b] The report is quoted as urging a surveillance and automated battle management system with weapons release control based on "predetermined, technically measurable conditions for engagement."[207] Without going into technical detail on the problem of predelegation—that is, relinquishing human decision-making authority to a preprogrammed battle management system[208]—it is difficult to envisage Congress or the public endorsing a strategic program that not merely limits but removes presidential control of weapons release.

Although the report is cited as being optimistic about the early development prospects for a list of emerging technologies that together would com-

---

[b]The 2,000 boosters probably refer to ICBM and SLBM (sea-launched ballistic missile) launchers.

prise the several BMD layers, and as noting that boost-phase kill devices would still be useful in attacking surviving postboost vehicles (that is, in attacking a greatly increased set of deployed reentry vehicle targets), it also states that there are no certain assessments of postboost vehicles supporting any projections of BMD systems vulnerability.[209] Despite the vagueness of this characterization, the Fletcher Report authors could be hinting that Soviet postboost vehicles could well be configured or programmed in such a way that their vulnerability to directed-energy weapons or nonnuclear kill devices will decrease as Soviet weapons designers react to the specific U.S. deployment decision. For reasons discussed later, ICBMs can be rendered more secure from and less vulnerable to directed-energy weapons through a number of relatively inexpensive countermeasures.

One major conclusion reached by *Aviation Week,* based on their reading of the Fletcher Report and their interpretation of state-of-the-art developments, is therefore not surprising: our ability to detect boost-phase launches with precision reduces the technical challenges to problems of survivability and endurance. *Aviation Week,* then, claims that sensor improvements to date render one of the principal obstacles to near-term deployment a nonproblem—once the detection and tracking system is nuclear-hardened and is given "autonomous signal and data processing" necessary to operate in the shorter wavelengths.[210]

As discussed earlier, however, one of the greatest difficulties posed by space-based BMD is the uncertainty surrounding the immature state of such detection, tracking, and pointing technologies. A few months before *Aviation Week* declared the basic space-based detection technology sound, General E.R. Heiberg, commander of the Army's BMD Command, was quoted as saying that the Defense Department was still "putting together" an experimental airborne optical adjunct sensor concept to identify, sort, and track incoming targets: "It is an optical approach that is largely untried, certainly in an airborne mode . . . we are in the middle of developing the concept."[211] General Heiberg is referring to an endoatmospheric system, one of the most advanced programs of its kind, and does not even mention exoatmospheric approaches. While dismissing the problems of systems-hardening against nuclear weapons effects and autonomous signal and data processing—two additional problems that promise no easy resolution—it is hardly conceivable that detection technologies are such that the basic knowledge and equipment are now "deployed."

In a follow-on article, *Aviation Week* notes that Westinghouse (among others) has begun research into hypervelocity electromagnetic railgun technology, the principal nonnuclear BMD weapon system now under developmental consideration. As the prime Army contractor, Westinghouse has taken the lead in such work and has reportedly achieved projectile velocities of 4.2 kilometers per second. Requirements for BMD missions, however, call for velocities of 25 kilometers per second and, at a minimum, must first achieve speeds of more than twice those achieved to date.[212] Again, it will be no simple task to devise a space-based railgun system that will be light enough to be lofted into orbit and powerful enough to achieve the requisite velocities. Important trade-offs would be necessary if a prototype weapon platform were pushed into early deployment—trade-offs that would seriously degrade even minimal performance requirements.

The article (and the series) concludes with an upbeat quotation from an anonymous "Pentagon official." Referring specifically to the Westinghouse-Army railgun development, but (one senses) equally applicable to the other advanced BMD concepts, the bureaucrat says that "the industry is limited only by the speed of light and engineering problems."[213] The editors of *Aviation Week,* through their anonymous official, are telling their influential readership that the sky is no longer the limit in the U.S. quest for power and prestige. To argue that only the speed of light and engineering obstacles stand in the way of seizing new horizons is in reality an admission that basic theoretical and technological difficulties remain: we are limited, it is suggested, only by our will and determination to proceed with a program.

Those at *Aviation Week* and elsewhere who favor the strategic defense initiative, as the incipient multilayered BMD plan is called by the administration, usually couch their enthusiasm in carefully crafted language replete with technical qualifiers. Apart from a small minority of true believers subscribing to General Graham's assertion that BMD technologies have by and large arrived, those responsible for persuading the president to embark on an extensive orbital defensive network with space-based technologies did so with strategic considerations uppermost in their minds. Advances in lasers, particle beams, sensors, and the like, had progressed incrementally, at best, between 1980 and the BMD decision in 1983—1980 being President Carter's last full year in office. That same year, Carter issued Presidential Directive (PD) 59, sometimes known as the "countervailing strategy," in addition to announcing plans to construct the advanced technology (Stealth) bomber. Why, then, wasn't a decision taken in 1980, a year in which several important strategic decisions were taken to bolster the old MAD system? The "technology pull" argument fails, in large part, because it does not tell us why a decision that could easily have been made in 1980 was not taken until a new administration decided to do so three years later.

The Carter philosophy, previously endorsed by Presidents Nixon and Ford, was set out as follows in his last defense budget (FY 1981):

> We recognize . . . that attempting to construct a complete defense against
> a massive Soviet nuclear attack would be prohibitively costly, destabilizing
> and in the end, almost certain to fail. And cost aside, the Anti-Ballistic

Missile (ABM) Treaty of 1972 and the 1974 Protocol restrict the deployment of ABM systems in order to prevent a futile damage-limiting competition.[214]

The principal Reagan defense advisors have from the first been hostile to MAD, SALT, and all the accompanying acronymic concepts brought forth by the age of offense-dominated deterrence. They shun MAD because, under its terms, one must accept parity (strategic equivalence) with Moscow. The 1980 Republican platform called for a resurgence in military spending to attain America's long-lost strategic superiority. In the nuclear era, however, there is only one way for either side to achieve meaningful superiority—through developing the means if feasible, to defend one's territory and military forces against opposing nuclear weapons.

The Reagan administration's initial rhetoric about regaining superiority was eventually toned down as a result of mounting criticism at home and abroad. There was a widespread perception in 1981 of U.S. bellicosity and unwillingness to engage in serious arms control talks, especially at the theater (or intermediate) nuclear level. Alliance leaders in Europe grew wary of U.S. actions and sought to distance themselves from talk of "nuclear warning shots" and the feasibility of protracted nuclear conflict.[c] The unveiling of President Reagan's "zero option" plan in November 1981, in which the scheduled deployment of U.S. Pershing II ballistic missiles and ground-launched cruise missiles would be forgone in exchange for Soviet elimination of their SS-20 intermediate-range missile force, defused much of the adverse criticism previously leveled at the administration. In the process, the principal U.S. decision makers learned that discussing military superiority in such unabashedly frank terms (as they did prior to November 1981) only served to frighten people and mobilize their opposition.

Still, many of the top appointees did not relinquish their longer-term objective of regaining superiority. As uncomfortable as ever with MAD (despite their strong support for MAD weapons systems such as the MX and the B-1 bomber—necessary as interim expedients to "close the window of vulnerability"), the Reagan national security officials could turn only to BMD as the preferred alternative to building more MAD systems, with increasingly limited support, or engaging in sustained arms control negotiations that ultimately reinforce nuclear parity and undermine the nation's will to pursue strategic defense.

There is no doubt that some technological basis for an advanced multilayered BMD system exists today, as it did in 1967 for a more limited ABM program. Then, as now, those arguing in favor of strategic defense

---

[c]In congressional testimony during the summer of 1981, former Secretary of State Alexander Haig spoke of firing nuclear warning shots as a possible response to a Soviet attack on Western Europe.

alluded to the near-term feasibility of their concept; doing otherwise would have undercut the impetus for moving forward with development today rather than tomorrow. As with ABM, however, the proponents of BMD are motivated first and foremost by the need to recapture military superiority—without stating it as such. Favorable technology estimates build support for a program whose real chances of success are unknowable or dismal. Referring to the ABM debate, Morton Halperin notes that optimistic Army and DARPA scientists were used by the JCS to marshal their arguments in favor of development: "A desire to make an effective case for a deployment led to underestimates of cost and overestimates of feasibility."[215] Yet the JCS and their congressional supporters presented the issue to President Johnson not in terms of technological wizardry but "in terms of the importance of maintaining American strategic nuclear superiority."[216]

Toward the end of November 1983, Secretary of Defense Weinberger reported that, after digesting the content of the Fletcher Report, the administration had agreed "in principle" to begin development of a long-term defensive program. Weinberger said that it was first necessary to achieve a "huge increase in computational capability" and a variety of other breakthroughs and improvements before a BMD network would be ready. The earliest operational start-up was described as "the very late end of this century or the beginning of the next."[217]

A number of prominent physicists echoed Weinberger's technological caution, and several went well beyond declarations of uncertainty to derisive hostility and ridicule. Hans Bethe of Cornell University, for example, said that, in his opinion, the exotic defense schemes are "still totally science fiction."[218] Kurt Gottfried (also of Cornell) and Sidney Drell, deputy director of the Stanford Linear Accelerator Center, were quoted as saying that "the aerodynamic and physical stresses would be difficult for the laser stations to withstand." The supercomputers necessary to control all the space-based components in an extremely compressed time frame must first be developed, along with numerous other materials and engineering advances now only in an early conceptual stage.[219] Donald Kerr, director of the Los Alamos National Laboratory, said in September 1983 that "at this point, in the main, they are physics concepts still to be proved,"[220] while Robert M. Bowman, director of Air Force strategic defense programs from 1976 to 1978 and now the president of the Institute for Space and Security Studies, has written that, despite the "many promising technologies that might" be produced, "there are monumental technological problems associated with each system."[221]

Prior to Secretary Weinberger's late-November announcement that a decision had been made to proceed "in principle," his under secretary for research and engineering (Richard DeLauer) testified at a hearing on Senator William Armstrong's bill to establish a unified space command and implement President Reagan's BMD concept. DeLauer said that "a workable defense" is twenty years away and that technology demonstrations will be very costly because each of the new technologies in demand will be equal to or more extensive than any Manhattan Project. At that same hearing, Hans Bethe testified that the requisite technologies are quite immature and will probably fail in their designated tasks. Bethe unfavorably compared the president's proposal to the Apollo program, testifying that the "fundamental principles" of the lunar landing concept were well understood, whereas this is not now the case with BMD.[222]

Following the Defense Department's assimilation of the Fletcher Report's findings, a decision was taken to proceed with new and increased funding in five broad research areas. In the FY 1985 defense budget submitted to the Congress on February 1, 1984, Secretary Weinberger requested $1.77 billion in R&D funding for the strategic defense initiative and an additional $226 million for associated "space defense" systems featuring ASAT and related C^3 development that could well be relevant to a future BMD deployment. The Pentagon budget document, following the guidance laid down in January 1984 in NSDD 119 (on strategic defense), offers an assessment of the initiative that is striking in its caution—particularly when viewed against the much headier optimism displayed by *Aviation Week*:

> Although numerous complex technical problems must be overcome, our preliminary studies conclude that an effective defense against ballistic missiles is potentially feasible. Major research and development efforts will be required in directed-energy weapons, conventional weapons, and surveillance and target acquisition systems.[223]

The Defense Department language makes it clear that the DeLauer wing of the Pentagon policy establishment prevailed over those advocating a more ambitious crash program. General Graham's High Frontier concept, entailing an early deployment of off-the-shelf, existing technologies, was deemed infeasible by those who ultimately would be responsible for developing the weapons and administering the program.

The excerpted portions of the Fletcher Report cited in *Aviation Week* raise a number of questions about the viability of a proposed multilayered BMD. Could such a system ever be built, or is it merely science fiction, as critiqued by Hans Bethe? Have numerous technological changes since the late 1960s made BMD more feasible today than ABM was then, and, if so, can it be argued that the arrival of new (though disparate) technologies forced the decision upon us?

Although there are obviously a number of separate paths to be taken, I will assume here that the administration is interested in pursuing an extensive, multilayered BMD network, extending from endoatmospheric terminal (or point) defense upward through several tiers of exoatmospheric defense. At least one of these tiers will be composed of directed-energy weapons (possibly including the nuclear-pumped X-ray laser), supplemented by nonnuclear kinetic energy hit-to-kill projectiles within the same tier or in another tier. The military objective of such an extensive network would be to destroy Soviet ICBMs during the boost phase of their flight (that is, before each missile deploys its complement of MIRVs) and, failing that, to intercept as many surviving warheads as possible during the remaining stages of flight (that is, the mid-course and terminal phases). To establish the role of technology in the Star Wars decision, analysts must ask if the information available to the president's principal advisors bespoke optimism or pessimism.

As noted earlier, a number of top presidential advisors have commented publicly on the relative immaturity of the BMD technologies in question both before and after the Star Wars speech of March 23, 1983. Such caution strongly implies that even classified information available only to a small inner circle of advisors did not hold out more than a glimmer of hope that a realistic system could be built and deployed before the end of the century. Occasional hints to the contrary in 1983 and early 1984 fell far short of the kind of technological understanding that predated the Apollo program decision—an example noted by Hans Bethe—and appeared to be aimed at the congressional budget committees whose funding authorizations are needed by the administration in order to proceed.

The variety of poorly understood BMD problems in question may be divided into two major categories: difficulties in *constructing* an integrated system that actually works, and difficulties in *defending* the system once it is deployed. In practice, the construction of any BMD network ought to factor in defensive measures, as suggested by the Fletcher Report; for purposes of discussion, however, the two will be treated as separate problems.

The two principal directed-energy candidates at the time of the decision were high-energy lasers (HELs) and charged particle beams (CPBs). Serious consideration was (and still is) given to nuclear-derived X-ray lasers, as proposed by Edward Teller through his Project Excalibur, and neutral particle beams. These proposed weapons concepts will be examined in turn, followed by a more general discussion of the vulnerabilities of these exotic systems. The vulnerabilities are vital to any BMD discussion because they allow us to assess the possible leverage, or cost-exchange ratio, granted by advanced BMD deployments (defined as a measure of the "outcome of competition between the defense to improve its performance and the offense to maintain penetrability,"[224] or, more simply, how much the USSR will spend to overcome our BMD compared to how much the United States will spend in developing and deploying it).

High-energy lasers as potential weapons operate on the principle that a strongly focused beam of light would thermally destroy a target either through a rapid series of pulses or through a continuous stream of electromagnetic waves. HELs would probably use a molecular gas as a medium, to which external energy must be supplied. Kosta Tsipis, a physicist at MIT, convened a workshop of university, industry, and weapons laboratory scientists in 1981 to examine the feasibility of lasers as weapons. His workshop "concluded that lasers have little or no chance of succeeding as practical, cost-effective weapons."[225]

Tsipis first describes the three revolutionary differences between HELs and present weapons systems:

> Beams of intensely amplified light are used to destroy objects, rather than explosives from reentry vehicles or artillery shells.

> The light energy would move at the speed of light (300 million meters/ second), compared to the much slower speed of supersonic ICBMs (at 1000–2000 meters/second).

> The laser must *directly* strike the target, whereas a nuclear explosive is effective over a much greater distance.

As the Fletcher Report recognized, the laser itself would be just one component of a laser BMD. A very large mirror is necessary for pointing, as are sensors to detect, identify, and determine the position of numerous targets; additional mirrors for damage assessment; control devices; and extensive energy storage and generating systems capable of emitting powerful pulses or waves at the desired moment. Ground-based energy-generating systems, though advantageous in regard to power supply, require still higher frequencies and larger aiming mirrors, because the laser will diffract as it moves through the atmosphere.[226] Daniel Kaplan of Battelle Pacific Northwest Laboratories points out that, beyond a certain distance, the intensity of power decreases "as the square of the distance from the source."[227] Either the power source generating the laser must be extremely powerful, or the distance between the ground or orbital battle station and the target must be kept minimal. This trade-off is crucial and must be factored into the final cost-exchange ratios. As a geometric expression, Kaplan's point also applies to lasers moving through a vacuum (exoatmospherically).

As Tsipis and other physicists note, a ground-based laser aimed either toward a space-based mirror (serving as a relay station to bounce or direct the beam toward an enemy warhead) or directly at an incoming target will encounter a number of serious obstacles. Atmospheric absorption of light will weaken the intensity of the pulse or wave—requiring virtually perfect weather or very small distances between the power-generating source and the reentry vehicle. Fog, rain, snow, smoke, dust, and cloudy weather will degrade the laser's theoretically smooth path, a phenomenon known as *scattering*. Another endoatmospheric problem is called *thermal blooming*, wherein the air in the beam heats up and expands. As the density of the air in and around the laser's path changes in its upward ascent, so also does the index of refraction, causing the beam to disperse.

Above the atmosphere, numerous problems remain. A target of highly polished aluminum struck by an infrared pulsed laser would absorb just 4 percent of the laser's radiation, and perhaps more (but still less than 10 percent) with a laser focusing radiation in the visible wavelengths. Ultraviolet radiation deposited on a target would be more lethal. Consider, however, the following difficulties involved in melting a metal surface several millimeters thick:

> 1,000 watts per square centimeter must be absorbed for one second (that is, the target must absorb a total energy of 1,000 joules per square centimeter) but, because of the posited high reflectivity of the target, an infrared laser must deliver 20,000 joules per square centimeter (since less than 5 percent of the radiation will be absorbed).

> More than 50 orbital laser battle stations at 1,000 kilometers above the earth's surface must be deployed in order to ensure continuous coverage of Soviet ICBM fields (it may be possible to deploy fewer stations at geosynchronous orbit,[d] but the requisite power levels would be enormous).

> Each laser battle station in this minimal deployment scenario must then be capable of destroying or disabling 1,400 Soviet missiles within the first 4 to 5 minutes of flight[e] under boost-phase intercept requirements, leaving less than 0.5 second for each intercept.

> To destroy each ICBM, ten pulses of several hundred millionths of a second duration will be required if the energy intensity focused on the target is 1 million watts per square centimeter (again, necessary because 5 percent or less will be absorbed).[228]

Taken together, these four points illustrate the unprecedented complexity presented by the advanced-BMD task. An example using the foregoing information is given by Tsipis. Assume that an operational hydrogen-fluoride pulsed laser with a 1-meter-diameter mirror received information from the

---

[d]Geosynchronous orbit is 22,300 miles above the earth. Although roughly 50 laser stations with 1,000-kilometer ranges would ensure that there would always be one station over the USSR, as many as 400 or more such stations may be necessary (mostly for the sake of redundancy). At geosynchronous orbit, Kaplan estimates that more than 200 stations would still be necessary.

[e]Tsipis uses the figure of 1,000 soviet missiles and 8 minutes for the duration of the boost phase, leaving about 0.5 second for each ICBM intercept.

battle station's sensors of an ascending Soviet ICBM wave. If we further assume, somewhat conservatively, that 10 percent of the laser's radiation will be absorbed on the target's surface, then 10,000 joules per square centimeter per pulse must be delivered. The beam must cover a target area of almost 8,000 square centimeters at a distance of 1,000 kilometers, so the area of the mirror must also be 8,000 square centimeters. The total energy generated, then, allowing for 10 percent absorption, must be about 80 million joules per pulse: "If the pulses were to last for roughly 100 microseconds, the power of the laser would be almost a million megawatts, which is quite unattainable."[229]

The hydrogen-fluoride laser used in the example would itself represent a major breakthrough if the requisite energy levels could only be scaled-up as *Aviation Week* desires. The two best potential laser concepts, in fact, are both hydrogen-fluoride lasers, the smaller system powered by 5 megawatts, with a 4-meter-diameter mirror, and the larger system powered by 10 megawatts, with a 10-meter mirror, according to Kaplan. Both concepts would be larger than present HELs by a substantial margin, "and the optics are not comparable in size and precision to any high-power mirror that has yet been built."[230]

It has been argued that a continuous-wave laser would be more lethal and would need less power to melt a hole in an ICBM. Tsipis estimates that 2-millimeter-thick aluminum will melt after absorption of 400 joules per square centimeter. If the reflectivity is again 90 percent (that is, only 10 percent radiation absorption), then a 100-megawatt carbon dioxide laser (far more powerful than the lasers described by Kaplan) would need about 100 seconds per target to damage the ICBM 1,000 kilometers distant. More important, each Soviet ICBM is *accelerating,* and we have allotted only 0.5 second per target.[231] The continuous-wave laser must therefore improve its lethality by a factor of 200—quite an unprecedented scaling-up effort.

How would such a laser battle station, utilizing very powerful energy-production systems and huge mirrors, be assembled and deployed? It would certainly not be on earth; there are no heavy-lift launch vehicles capable of providing sufficient thrust, given the likely size of the payloads. Depending on the size of the mirrors, energy systems, and associated equipment, preliminary estimates range between a low of 100,000 pounds and a high of 500,000 pounds that must be lifted into orbit in successive stages, requiring many successive space shuttle launches.[232] Kaplan estimates that an adequate laser-BMD force, with each station weighing 100 tons, could be placed aloft after 14,000 shuttle flights. NASA, however, has planned fewer than 400 flights through 1992,[233] most of which are scheduled to carry payloads already chartered for other uses. If the NASA shuttle schedule were advanced significantly, and all uses other than BMD assembly were postponed—both improbable—it would still be at least another 30 years before a minimally feasible BMD network could be deployed and declared operable.

The minimal BMD force with ranges of 1,000 kilometers would only be able to guarantee that a very small fraction of battle stations would pass over Soviet territory at any one time. It would therefore be incumbent upon each individual laser station to be able to destroy the entire Soviet ICBM force. Planning of this sort obviously requires close to perfect efficiencies. Lasers currently operating in experimental laboratories or in industry possess efficiencies measured in single-digit percentages. Although it is possible for lasers eventually to attain 30 to 40 percent efficiencies, the energy-staging system "can at best reach 30 percent efficiency."[234] Because of the requirement that each station must possess enough power (and therefore fuel) to hit more than 1,000 Soviet ICBMs, an additional 1,000 shuttle flights will be required simply to provide enough fuel for energy storage alone.[235] Even these rough estimates are conservative, because the combination of one-third laser efficiencies coupled with one-third energy-generating efficiencies leads to the conclusion that fuel storage space aboard the station must be increased by at least a factor of ten, and more likely a factor of thirty.

A host of additional construction and operational problems related to directed-energy weapons, and lasers in particular, will only be briefly touched on here. Technologies as yet undeveloped cover all major aspects of the system, including verification of kills, supercomputers for battle management, sensing and tracking capabilities far more complicated and efficient than those now under development, and so on. Analogies to present weapons abound, but the essential problem has been well put by an anonymous Pentagon weapons planner, who likened the laser problem to "being on top of the Washington Monument, shooting a rifle, and hitting a baseball on top of the Empire State Building."[236] The "baseball" in the real world of BMD defense versus ICBM offense will be moving rather quickly, however, and will do its utmost to avoid being hit. In this context, some discussion must be devoted to the countermeasures open to Soviet ICBM engineers.

ICBMs that will some day face the danger of a concerted BMD can be prepared today to face those dangers with a high degree of confidence. The surfaces can be highly polished, as mentioned earlier, or mirrored, which would greatly limit the radiation absorption that would otherwise be suffered. Ablative coatings could readily be applied, increasing the reentry vehicle's hardening to 20,000 joules per square centimeter from 7,000 joules per square centimeter today. A layer of fluid in the missile's skin would deflect or absorb much of the laser's radiant energy, allowing the ICBM to continue its flight unimpaired. Missiles can also be programmed to rotate during flight, thereby distributing the hostile beam over a greater surface area and increasing its hardness by a factor of three.[237] The ICBM's engines may also be switched off earlier than they otherwise would be, thus reducing still further the time available to the BMD's directed-energy weapons to focus their beams or pulses. All these inexpensive countermeasures, by themselves, ensure that the cost-exchange ratio between defense and offense will overwhelmingly favor the offense. If one factors in the many inefficiencies and uncertainties related to tracking, discriminating between real and decoy targets, building and fueling a sufficiently powerful weapon, focusing the beam, devising mirrors far more durable and larger than any conceived to date (the diameters on large mirrors today are less than six feet), then the ratio worsens appreciably.

The ratio worsens yet again when one considers the tasks posed by defending the BMD network. Space-based directed-energy weapons will be vulnerable throughout the various assembly stages, or after full deployment, from a variety of sources. The many sensors and sensitive electronics comprising the C^3I elements can easily be blinded, jammed, or spoofed—as well as destroyed—by space mines, nuclear weapons detonations, or nonnuclear projectiles. The large optics necessary for powerful lasers hinder reliable self-defense because of the ease with which these larger targets can be destroyed by a massed attack of high-speed projectiles.[238] Communications links between laser stations, or between the lasers and ground-based controls under a space-ground system, will also be easily disrupted—especially in the latter network—because of the probable consequences of nuclear-induced electromagnetic pulse. Particle beams, discussed briefly later, are especially sensitive to nuclear detonations; a nuclear explosion in the upper atmosphere could push the ionosphere at that point into space, destroying the vacuum needed for a charged particle beam to travel through.

Particle beams pose a number of problems similar to lasers, especially in regard to defense of the battle station. Extremely powerful particle accelerators must be lifted into space, or assembled there, requiring magnitudinally similar construction and deployment problems. As nuclear accelerators appear to be the most cost-effective, deploying them in space to power the beam may raise questions about U.S. adherence to the Outer Space Treaty of 1967 (although probably not in technical violation). Nonnuclear-powered energy-generating systems would be enormous and would drive up the costs of the entire BMD program considerably.

Charged particle beams present a further difficulty, known as the *cathode effect*. If the beam targeted at the ICBM or reentry vehicle is composed of electrons, or negative charges, then there will be a correspondingly large build-up of protons, or positive charges. Such a charge build-up can cause the electrons to reverse course and damage the accelerator, rather than the ICBM it is supposed to attack. Charged particle beams must also have a very narrow radius for precise accuracy. As the beam homes in on the target in a boost-phase scenario, however, the earth's magnetic field will bend the beam; a 1 billion electron-volt electron traveling a distance of 1,000 kilometers will thus be bent by 100 to 200 kilometers. Allowing for correction, which is feasible up to a certain level, the uncertainty will still hover in the 100-meter range. Particle beams and lasers, unfortunately, must strike their targets directly. Neutral particle beams have been touted as a workable substitute, but the neutral beams tend to disperse more than the charged beams, and they cannot at this stage be as readily created or controlled.[239] This is not to argue that the cathode effect or the tendency for neutral particle beams to disperse cannot be rectified, only that many uncertainties remain and that operational weapons are completely unrealistic at this stage.

Finally, Professor Teller's X-ray laser, driven by a nuclear explosion, suffers from the aforementioned flaws in addition to its cost-ineffectiveness. The plan calls for a series of satellites to be launched into space upon warning of Soviet attack. The nuclear detonation would channel X rays through 40 to 50 "laser rods," which in turn would be aimed at a "footprint" in space through which Soviet missiles must travel to strike the United States. Each battle station, as may be observed, can be used only once. In addition, the project relies to a great extent on ground-to-space communications, which can be readily disrupted, and would still face all the tracking, discriminating, and accuracy challenges of other laser concepts.

The X-ray laser, in particular, would violate Article I of the Limited Test Ban Treaty of 1963 and Article IV of the Outer Space Treaty of 1967, which respectively limit exoatmospheric nuclear detonations and the emplacement in orbit of "any objects carrying nuclear weapons or any other kinds of weapons of mass destruction."[240] All advanced BMD systems would violate the ABM Treaty of 1972, Article V of which specifically limits the development, testing, or deployment of missile defense systems and components that are sea-based, air-based, *space-based,* or mobile land-based. Agreed Statement D of the ABM Treaty, referring to "other physical principles" that may be developed in the future, in no way countermands the provisions of Article V. In all, eight agreements or treaties would be violated by BMD and ASAT development or deployments.[241] Treaty violations aside, a space-based BMD would not cover depressed-trajectory SLBM, bombers, and air- or sea-launched cruise missiles, and a more extensive multilayered BMD would be severely strained to intercept a large volume of all these threats simultaneously.

The Star Wars decision, then, may be seen as a series of decisions, the first of which was taken shortly before the president's March 23 speech. In the following months, a second decision was taken to study the technological and security bases for BMD, resulting in the Fletcher and Hoffman reports of October 1983. A third decision was made toward the end of November 1983, based on the merger of the Fletcher and Hoffman studies. That decision committed the Reagan administration "in principle," to proceed with the "strategic defense initiative." A fourth and final decision was taken thereafter in regard to the defense budget for FY 1985, in which funding levels to begin an accelerated BMD program were set and officially promulgated on February 1, 1984.

The Reagan vision, in fact, allows for any combination of technological approaches to solve the problem of space-based defense. Reagan, Keyworth, Weinberger, and other BMD proponents have said, at times, that present technologies are such as to allow a serious BMD program to be realized over time, while at other times they have recited or acknowledged the long litany of physical and technological unknowns that can be resolved only through intensive examination. The president's doctrinal dissatisfaction with MAD, his discomfort with the history and present status of strategic arms control, and his desire to return the United States to nuclear superiority convinced him of the need to channel military R&D toward new, untried, and unproven defensive concepts (especially space-based directed-energy weapons). Significantly, strategic emphasis is not being shifted immediately away from offensive weapons production supportive of MAD.

The BMD defense decision of 1983 represents the beginning of a wholly new direction in U.S. strategic policy. Although ABMs of limited characteristics and missions have been contemplated since the late 1950s, none were incorporated into U.S. doctrine or force structure except as a minor adjunct to the ABM Treaty of 1972. The 100 land-fixed interceptors and associated large radars allowed under the treaty were never fully deployed by the United States, and even that small network was dismantled in 1975. If doctrine, policies, and weapons were to shift toward strategic defense and away from deterrence, as they are now doing (though gradually and by no means decisively), the strategic environment of the 1990s and the twenty-first century would be radically different from that shaped by the men responsible for the atomic and hydrogen bomb decisions.

The super debate of 1949–1950 and the Star Wars debate of 1983–1984 share many similarities but have several differences, some of which will be discussed in detail in the concluding chapter. In addition to the relationship between these two case studies and the problem of causation in the Soviet-American arms race, a further question arises from the likely consequences of the two decisions examined in this study (particularly the latter, for its topical relevance). We must also ask whether both superpowers are readying their militaries, their arsenals, and their peoples for a qualitatively new cycle of the arms race, and whether the future competition on earth and in space will bring us closer to assured survival or assured destruction.

Strategic Implications

Concepts like space-based lasers for ABMs require only imagination and can be seductive, but they remain only concepts. . . . Concepts invite easy manipulation of numbers with only slight reference to reality.
—Jack Ruina, 1981[242]

The preceding analysis has contended that strategic weapons choices are best understood "in the political and institutional context in which decisions are made," and not primarily as a result of technological momentum or drive.[243] Jack Ruina's point should be carefully read: concepts are not physical or engineering facts, and those that say otherwise have other motivations in mind. For Harry Truman and Dean Acheson, the underlying concept was deterrence of the newly acquired Soviet atomic capability through bigger and more destructive weapons with which to better threaten retaliation. The U.S. atomic monopoly having been shattered, Truman sought to regain superiority (believed lost by the Soviets' very possession of atomic bombs) through a strengthened thermonuclear stockpile.

Ronald Reagan's concept would fundamentally undermine Truman's premise of deterrence. Defensive weapons feasibility must be pursued, his administration believes; if advancing the prospects of the technological concept wins support in Congress and among the public, then "manipulation of numbers" may help bring the president's vision closer to reality.

The two decisions bear a striking resemblance to one another, apart from the premise of this book that the basic technologies and much of the fundamental physics were not in place at the time each decision was made. No one, not even Professor Teller, had any clear notion of how to go about designing and building a viable weapon in 1949–1950. Attention was focused on other aspects of military technology—most notably, increasing the size of the weapon yield. The directed-energy weapons of tomorrow that would form the centerpiece of an advanced, multilayered BMD were similarly in a state of incipient conceptualization prior to President Reagan's March 23 speech. Progress had been achieved across many technical fronts, but the prospects of an integrated, feasible approach were dim in 1983 (and little better in 1984). There was no real BMD program to speak of, just as there was no hydrogen bomb program, before the president focused national attention on the issue and called for a major effort to be made.

A second similarity relates to the manner in which key policy officials from both the executive and the legislative branches—as well as a number of science advisors—believed that a military solution was preferable to a diplomatic or political solution. The tendency of proponents in both decisions to declare that their concept would eliminate, once and for all, hostile threats aimed at the United States was quite pronounced. Oppenheimer was concerned in 1949 that those favoring the super's development actually believed that the hydrogen bomb would provide a blanket "answer to the problems posed by the Russian advance." McMahon and others argued in terms that bore out Oppenheimer's judgment. Similarly, General Graham of High Frontier has stated time and again that his Global Ballistic Missile Defense not only will eliminate the Soviet nuclear threat but will also pave the way for U.S. industrialization of space. Both military and industrial concerns may then be brushed aside.

David Lilienthal, Truman's chairman of the AEC, feared that the super would make the "prospects for peace less good." He argued, further, that the hydrogen bomb offered no nonmilitary by-product, that it was "straight gadget making." It is unclear whether policymakers within the Reagan administration who opposed the strategic defense initiative made like arguments, but many critics outside the government have countered the High Frontier space industrialization claims as a transparent effort to gain support for their program through the lure of lucrative technology spin-offs that are yet to be developed. There is a tenuous link at best, critics say, between the various BMD concepts now being put forward for consideration and feasible industrial workshops in space. The links in question—for example heavy-lift launch vehicles and manned space stations—in no way depend on BMD deployments in order to proceed.

Both debates shared a strong budgetary component. The economics of building a new array of heretofore unknown weapons systems worried many of the participants in the hydrogen bomb decision, especially in relation to the strongly held beliefs of Kennan and members of the GAC. They particularly feared the implications for Western defense policy should the weapon prove feasible and be deployed en masse, believing that the new production commitment would dictate unsound strategies and would be very costly. Critics of the Star Wars concept likewise reject the change in strategy, as they do the financial burden imposed by advanced BMD. The highest of these cost estimates is given by MIT physicist George Rathjens, who put the cost at $500 billion for a "baseline" system exclusive of additional funding required for support, counter-countermeasures, and the like.[244] The cost estimates given by the Fletcher Report amount to one-fifth of Rathjens' estimates.

A fourth similarity can be found in the debate over each system's military effectiveness and the respective cost-benefit (or cost-exchange) ratios, the latter related to the aforementioned economic burden. Kennan, Lilienthal, and Oppenheimer did not believe that the super would add any significant deterrent potential to the fission bomb program, nor would U.S. possession of the super make the United States more militarily defensible. The costs involved in proceeding with an ambitious super program were not justified, they stressed, by the increments to retaliatory capacity thereby gained. Opponents of the space-based defense concept similarly argued in 1983 that its probable military effectiveness would be extraordinarily low for the foreseeable future, and that the developmental and operational costs associated with deployment were therefore much better spent elsewhere. Tsipis, Rathjens, and others have argued that the leak rate (that is, the number of re-entry vehicles that would survive the BMD net) would be enormous both for urban and for point or terminal defense. High levels of BMD funding may also cut into other military spending that would be equally if not more valuable.

A fifth connection between the two debates is the role of the technical fix in decision makers' perceptions. The technical fix is often sought by those faced with a particularly vexing political challenge. It must not be construed as a process or a piece of hardware waiting in the wings to force itelf upon inert politicians. Rather, the technical fix is usually just another concept that, in the world of defense priorities, fulfills a doctrinal need *in theory*. More often than not—even for conventional weapons programs—the technical fix proves to be illusory, short-lived, and at best a poor substitute for creative strategy and tactics.

In 1949, David Lilienthal argued that development of more powerful weapons, such as the thermonuclear device, was just such a deceptive technical fix; he said that people would then believe that the bigger bombs in the U.S. arsenal would provide them with security when in fact "none exists." Weapons with very great destructive yield may or may not add to our ability to deter war, but in either case they cannot guarantee absolute security. Lilienthal led the assault on the super, based in large part on his belief that only negotiations to achieve strict limitations on (if not the complete elimination of) nuclear weapons could provide mutual security. Otherwise, he feared that an expensive and dangerous arms race would ensue, threatening to worsen the national security of both the United States and the USSR.

Today, ardent proponents of space-based defense aver that absolute security can be achieved through a military reversion to the basic principles of strategic defense. The military's mission has been justified historically in many democracies as territorial (and sometimes allied) defense and then, later, as defense of national interests overseas. The postwar mission changed only the manner in which territorial defense was to be executed, in that deterrence of nuclear war through a constant offensive threat substituted for the more traditional meaning of defense as merely warding off an adversary's attack—without threatening attack in return. In practice, however, the theory of pure defense has rarely been utilized by organizations and societies larger than hunter-gatherers; defending one's territory and interests has most often combined offensive capability with Maginot Lines and strong fortifications.

The Reagan administration, in pursuing a people-oriented strategic defense in conjunction with the more limited goals of defending important military targets (that is, a combined population and terminal defense), has opted for building a Maginot Line in space that would eventually be comprehensive in coverage. The stated objective is a gradual substitution of defensive for offensive forces. Like Senator McMahon, Secretary of Defense Johnson, and AEC Commissioner Lewis Strauss in 1949, the Reagan administration believes that the new program will one day provide total security—whereas critics such as Lilienthal 35 years ago or Hans Bethe today have countered that security of this sort is a dangerous illusion.

A sixth relationship flows directly from the fifth: pursuit of the ultimate weapon (either offensive, as in 1949, or defensive, as in 1983) moves the superpowers either one step further from a potentially beneficial arms control arrangement or one step closer to peace through strength. Critics of both decisions contend the former, while supporters cling to the latter of these two formulations. The critics asserted, as did Lilienthal in 1949, that the arms race between Moscow and Washington would be intensified "in a new way." The relationship would grow increasingly unstable as the opportunity to seek an arms agreement rapidly dissipated. The instability would be engendered by a series of escalatory R&D investments, building one upon the other, in an effort to attain new counterweapons set off by the initial feasibility and production decisions. Arms control, charge the critics, works best when it seeks to prevent potentially destabilizing concepts from being actualized into proliferated weapons systems.

Those favoring the decisions argued that revolutionary new weapons designs were a better guarantor of peace than negotiating with an avowed enemy with whom one could not trust to keep agreements. Secretary Johnson so argued in 1949, backed by the JCS and many factions within the government who believed that negotiations with Moscow were probably dangerous and in the end would prove useless. In 1983, Secretary of Defense Weinberger (supported by Teller) followed the tenets of the 1980 Republican Party platform, which viewed the SALT process as a powerful tranquilizer inducing complacency among the public in regard to the Soviet threat. According to this view, negotiations had strongly favored Moscow in the past; the implication was that in the Reagan years, arms control would only proceed on terms that restored the former imbalance by favoring Washington. Rebuilt military strength across the board and the pursuit of advanced weapons were perceived as the surest way to contain the military ambition of the Soviet leadership.

A final link between the two decisions is provided by Edward Teller. Teller lobbied hard for the super in 1949, after the nation heard the news of the Soviet nuclear breakthrough. He galvanized fellow scientists Lawrence, Alvarez, and Von Neumann and spent a great deal of time with congressmen and national security officials arguing that only superior nuclear strength would deter Soviet military action. He did not claim that the hydrogen bomb was a certainty, only that we must embark on an experimental program to determine its feasibility. If the United States did not undertake the task, he warned, the Soviet Union certainly would.

More recently, Teller has agitated for a number of years against the world of MAD in favor of an elaborate system of advanced directed-energy concepts that would comprise a ballistic missile defense against Soviet strategic weapons. He believes BMD offers more hope for the United States and is a more humane military mission than a threat of wanton destruction. One of the major candidates for space-based BMD is Professor Teller's Project Excalibur. Teller's critics have noted, as John Manley did in 1949, that his enthusiasm for the project and the larger concept have outrun his professional judgment as a physicist.

The H-bomb and Star Wars decisions, alike as they are, differed in three salient respects. First, President Truman called for a feasibility test, looking toward a crash program if the technology should prove within grasp. Almost immediately, the Defense Department pushed for a production schedule—well in advance of the feasibility program. The Defense Department administrators reasoned that if the hydrogen bomb *could* be built, an early decision on production would strengthen their hand as they called for the new weapon's rapid assimilation into the growing nuclear arsenal.

President Reagan, on the other hand, has paid homage to the twin facts of strong resistance against BMD and the technological challenges inherent in his elaborate plan. He has asked only that we accelerate R&D, recognizing that a crash program would be infeasible because of the much longer development and procurement lead times that differentiate strategic weapons procurement today from the earlier, initial postwar process. It also remains to be seen whether the strategic defense initiative will resemble the comprehensive territorial shield described in the March 23 speech or will be more limited in scope, and this in part detracts from an ambitious crash program because different missions will dictate different systems. Secretary Weinberger left little doubt, shortly after the Star Wars speech, that the president's intentions are indeed grandiose: "The defensive systems the President is talking about are not designed to be partial." Weinberger also mentioned that the administration wanted a system that would be "thoroughly reliable" as well as "total."[245] The Hoffman Report recommends, however, that "intermediate options" protecting only critical military assets would be desirable even if a full-scale deployment cannot occur.[246]

A second difference is apparent in the ethical or moral foundation of to-day's debate compared with the relative lack of moral suasion used in 1949–1950. The only participants who raised moral concerns were members of the GAC—Fermi and Rabi had written that the super was "necessarily an evil thing in any light"—and their arguments were met with intense hostility from Senator McMahon, who believed that their ethical recommendation was a breach of their position and authority as technical, not theological, advisors.

Since 1981, the churches and many lay groups became passionately involved with nuclear weapons issues, most strongly advising the Reagan administration to devise serious arms control proposals. Churches were early supporters of the nuclear freeze movement, both in Western Europe in 1981 and in the United States in 1982. Thus, the Reagan speech of March 23, 1983, and subsequent administration pronouncements stressed the superior moral commitment in strictly defending one's territory as against the more onerous task of deterring through nuclear threats of mass destruction. The focus of the Reagan plan, however, to defend the United States and our allies through the emplacement of a new generation of weapons in orbit, was immediately attacked in the press and in Congress and derisively labeled "Star Wars." It remains to be seen whether the president will convince supporters of the nuclear freeze to abandon their faith in the 1972 ABM Treaty—the one arms limitation treaty universally applauded by arms controllers as truly effective and stabilizing.

A final difference between the two decisions is the role played by doctrine. In 1950, President Truman did not possess a clear notion of how the new weapon would fit into military doctrine or force structure, and neither did most of his key civilian and military advisors. The Pentagon believed, in a general sense, that the hydrogen explosive would prove more militarily useful, but their arguments on this score were not particularly strong. Rather, they felt (as did Truman and Acheson) that political necessity left them no choice, that the public would not tolerate a decision to forgo a super weapon that Moscow might pursue, and that the new bomb would somehow afford the United States greater leverage in world affairs. A suitable doctrinal justification would be found *after* feasibility testing, when the weapon's parameters were better understood.

In 1983, when President Reagan decided to redirect research priorities into strategic defense, the Defense Department and the Office of Science and Technology Policy within the Executive Office of the President knew exactly where BMD would fit into doctrine if it should prove feasible and be carried to its furthest logical extension (that is, complete U.S. and allied leak-proof coverage). In the Reagan scheme, BMD was sought precisely because it can fulfill a doctrinal requirement that is conspicuously absent from the post-1950 deterrence-through-MAD system. Both political and military aspirations are directly addressed, through seeking to overturn deterrence as practiced today, with defense against all possible threats as the promise of tomorrow. Should BMD not be deployed in its most extensive, multilayered mode, active defenses will still be pressed into service to supplement deterrence by way of complicating a Soviet nuclear attack. Doctrine, in short, is ready for BMD.

It is often interesting for the specialist in national security affairs to compare defense decisionmaking over time, thereby gauging changes in style and substance. Despite the vast differences between the worlds of Truman and Reagan, more similarities are present in these two decisions than one might initially suspect. The resemblance in thought, spanning a generation of major arms decisions, belies an important yet very simple lesson of the arms race: if the same mistake can be made again, institutional amnesia will ensure that eventually it will be made.

The irony is that mistakes need not be made if the thesis of this book is sound—that we call forth ever more destabilizing weapons systems through political choice, not through an uncontrollable, relentless march of advancing technology, as is popularly believed by so many. *Mistakes*, of course, is a subjective term in this context, and I realize full well that justice cannot be done to an analysis lacking in historical sensitivity. There may be more of a tragic element at work than I have given credence to in the hydrogen bomb decision, or perhaps there simply was "no other way," as President Truman so evidently believed. Notwithstanding Soviet behavior following World War II (justly characterized as opportunistic and at times brutal), however, there was such little empathy for the idea that a workable arms control agreement could be achieved or should be sought—at a time when there was unquestioned U.S. nuclear superiority—that it appears in retrospect a grave error not to have at least considered a moratorium on new and advanced weapons R&D or deployment.

Retrospect is easily gained, however, and provides cold comfort if one is proved correct (if that can ever really be done). Yet there were participants in the 1949–1950 debate who urgently called for an indefinite postponement of feasibility testing—Lilienthal, Kennan, Oppenheimer, Rabi, and Smyth, to name but a few—to investigate, first, the prospects for a mutual control arrangement between Moscow and Washington. They carefully considered the future and recoiled in horror as they contemplated an endless arms race in which the stakes would continually be raised. Can those who supported the initial decision to investigate the hydrogen atom's secrets for military use honestly submit that the world is now a safer place? There is considerable merit in the notion that there is no better time to negotiate than when one enjoys an advantage. In the case of the hydrogen bomb decision, our advantage lay in our superior nuclear strength, our superior conventional strength in many parts of the world, our unlimited strengths in science and technology, our robust economy, and our political and societal creativity.

Refinements in weapons yields, targeting accuracy, C³I, and a variety of other necessary and integrative strategic components have been the fruits of more than thirty years of unbridled nuclear weapons production subsequent to the first hydrogen bomb test. There is no sure guarantee that the past three decades would have been any different had we actively sought to reach an agreement with Moscow in 1950 banning thermonuclear weapons deployments, but we do know that the absence of an arms control effort then did not lead to a stable nuclear environment today. The absoluteness of that decision, regarding the putative power offered by hydrogen weaponry, is difficult to accept. If we can create weapons of untold destruction, then why can't we create counterweapons to eliminate the threat?

This was exactly the question raised in the first ABM debate of 1967–1969, and it has now become President Reagan's and Secretary Weinberger's question in 1983–1984. For reasons discussed in chapter 8, it is apparent that such complicated defenses as the president envisages are many years off and may well never be realized. The pursuit of these defenses has now begun in earnest, however, and it is crucial at this early stage in their development that we assess, as best we can, some of the major strategic implications looming ahead.

The strategic defense initiative is preferred by the Reagan administration because it is more appealing than protracted arms control negotiations. The key policy advisors, including such unofficial participants as Edward Teller, are convinced that only negotiations that restore the perceived imbalance of strategic forces (now favoring Moscow, in their view) ought to proceed. Despite protestations to the contrary, the Reagan proposals emphasizing major cuts in heavy land-based ICBMs can only have, first (and thus far have only had), the effect of inducing Soviet nonparticipation in the Strategic Arms Reduction Talks (START) round of negotiations. This is so because roughly 75 percent of Soviet strategic-nuclear power is invested in a land-based ICBM force, compared to 20 percent for the United States. Recent administration proposals for building more flexibility into the U.S. negotiating position do little to alter the essential thrust of the initial emphasis given to first reducing land-based heavy missiles by a substantial margin. Although most can agree that reductions of the scope sought by President Reagan are indeed desirable, in that they cut into the size and power of potential counterforce weapons (that is, weapons targeted against opposing nuclear and other critical military forces), it remains true that Moscow will not easily yield its most crucial military option without corresponding reductions in what the Soviets perceive to be key U.S. nuclear strengths.

The conclusion one is left with can only be that realistic arms control between the superpowers cannot move forward unless Moscow is prepared to make major concessions, concessions that have not been forthcoming to date. If the administration believes this as well, then it faces (as it did from the very first) an unfortunate dilemma: arms control talks are anathema, yet there is little doubt that the public is anxious over the lack of such talks and very much favors new arms agreements if they are considered fair to both sides. Moscow's refusal to negotiate on these grounds thus allows the administration to argue that it is the USSR that does not want to reach an agreement, while laying the groundwork in the battle for public opinion to pursue a number of offensive and defensive strategic arms programs. A Senate requirement to release periodic Soviet treaty violations further bolsters the administration's case that Moscow cannot be trusted to keep signed agreements, as an administration report in early 1984 listed violations pertaining to renewed BMD efforts on a more expansive scale.

The strategic defense initiative must therefore be viewed as part of an administration pattern of strategic decisions favoring arms acquisitions over arms control. The initiative fits in well with the policy refinements begun with P.D. 59 in 1980, moving, however, well beyond that approach toward a strategy of war-fighting that will some day feature arms-depriving weapons platforms as a central element. Pursuing a serious BMD network can only have the effect of worsening the chances for a more stable strategic climate through arms control, both because it raises the specter of a wholesale abrogation of some of the most effective treaties now in operation and because it will inevitably lead to leadership perceptions that the other side's BMD is superior in quality and, therefore, that more needs to be done to keep pace. Mutual suspicions and doubts are thus reinforced and multiplied, providing a new set of incentives to add rather than delete major weapons systems. The first strategic consequence, then, is a retreat from arms control, made acceptable by the chimera of ballistic missile defense.

A second consequence is the acceleration of a number of trends that worsen crisis stability. Predelegation of weapons release authority becomes necessary as the time allotted to make monumental decisions diminishes. The advent of very high speed data processing may not be immune from electromagnetic pulse disruption regardless of hardening levels, threatening the ever-tenuous communications links between satellites and, one day, weapons in space and their control stations on earth. Any combination of systems failures could trigger unwanted predelegation, in which instance Soviet communications or early-warning satellites could be attacked—alerting the Soviet Strategic Rocket Forces to what will surely look like a U.S. preemptive assault. Launch on warning of attack will be strengthened as a Soviet policy,[a] rather than launch on assessment (wherein the first wave of missile bursts over or on one's territory is positively certified).

---

[a]Launch on warning is believed by many strategic analysts to be official Soviet policy, but this, too, is open to differing interpretations.

The kind of active defenses sought by President Reagan will also have a bearing on the future strategic environment. A comprehensive BMD, one that is virtually leak-proof, will embolden leaders possessing such weapons to take risks they otherwise would not take. This applies even more to the Soviet Union. If both superpowers should embark upon "high-confidence" BMD systems that satisfy the core values of each leadership (that is, the United States may have a BMD geared more toward a population defense and the USSR may have one geared more toward silo defense), and if each country should feel that numerous simulations and tests prove their defensive weapons to be "thoroughly reliable," as Mr. Weinberger hopes, then conventional attacks or even limited nuclear strikes would become more realizable in the planners' minds.

The reality will be different for many years, however. Neither side can possibly deploy a BMD capable of providing a remotely acceptable defense in the foreseeable future. A further consequence will come, though, in the form of an accelerated spur to the arms race in space. The U.S. claims that the Soviets are considering a breakout from the ABM Treaty through a series of recent deployments of phased-array radars and new interceptor missiles with double the older system's range fuel the arguments of BMD proponents in Washington, despite the marginal defensive increments gained and the greater likelihood that these new capabilities are designed to limit damage from NATO tactical or theater systems. The spirit of the ABM Treaty may well have been violated, but the U.S. response thus far has been to push ahead with BMD and eventual resignation from the treaty, rather than actively seeking to ameliorate the treaty regime through the Standing Consultative Commission designed for such purposes.

Similarly, Soviet commentary pointing to the new U.S. military space programs, from ASAT to directed-energy BMD, strengthens the hands of those within the Soviet PRO (Anti-Missile Defense Force) and their bureaucratic allies to match or counter the new generation of U.S. weapons. Efforts in the weapons laboratories of both superpowers will be bolstered by the requirements engendered by BMD to overcome and penetrate the system. Passive measures to counter advanced BMD were described briefly in chapter 8; many new strategems will be added as development proceeds. Active measures threaten to add new categories and absolute numbers of space weapons to U.S. and Soviet inventories, from which the United States stands to lose more than the Soviet Union does because of the much greater U.S. reliance on satellite command-and-control of our globally dispersed forces. Offensive weapons systems will thus proliferate, complicating the defensive mission substantially while reducing still further the stability of the present deterrence regime.

A final consideration must be the type of BMD deployed and the missions it will be designed to accomplish. If future administrations decide to limit their objectives and pursue only a terminal defense against reentry vehicles in their final phase, then the defensive option (against ICBM silos and launch-control centers, not against cities) becomes more achievable, though how much more and at what cost remain uncertain. In this instance, however, we are not discussing any meaningful deviation from MAD. The preservation of the second-strike principle will remain intact. A more ambitious scheme, the kind envisaged by the president and his top advisors in the Star Wars speech, is much more problematical. How much more deterrence is bought by deploying a system of 90 percent efficiency over a system of 30 percent efficiency? Have we really eliminated the threat of a Soviet first strike, or have we merely provided Moscow with the incentive to chip away at the system's kill-rate?

Unless BMD is leak-proof, the argument of deterrence versus defense is actually one of some damage limitation versus no damage limitation—but within the confines of the world of mutual assured destruction. Rather than neatly complicating a Soviet nuclear attack and thus making it more distant, an inefficient BMD network must lead to increased crisis instability and a degradation in the admittedly imperfect system of deterrence—without substituting *real* defense for nuclear offense in the strategic calculus.

If BMD is to be utilized primarily to defend the U.S. retaliatory ICBM force—deemed necessary because of that force's alleged vulnerability to a Soviet first strike—then it is a poor choice given its probable vulnerabilities when compared with the options of combined mobility and silo or launcher hardening. Arms accords designed to reduce heavy warhead yields and numbers of deliverable weapons will greatly supplement such an approach. Rather than force Moscow to replace their heavy missile force with smaller, single-warhead ICBMs, BMD instead compels the Soviet Union to *improve* and add to the most effective element of their strategic deterrent (SS-17s, SS-18s, SS-19s, and possible fifth-generation heavy ICBMs).

One can only speculate on the underlying or hidden motivations of the administration in regard to BMD. There appears to be a large faction, to which I would assign the president and nearly all of his key advisors, that sincerely believes that technical problems will be overcome, that deterrence will actually be strengthened, and that strategic defense promises a bright new world for mankind. A smaller part of that faction, however, perhaps realizes that it will be several decades, at least, before all the pieces are in place for the sort of extensive BMD currently desired. An interim goal, however, in the form of a sophisticated ASAT program, is lent greater credence by initial funding for BMD R&D. In the FY 1985 allocations, there is much that is applicable to ASAT development: limited-power lasers; C^3I assets; and pointing, tracking, and discrimination technologies. BMD may not have significant civilian spin-off potential, but it appears to be well suited to supplementing present ASAT efforts. Congressional sentiment against ASAT development and deployment may not extend to R&D funds for BMD, because ASATs are an imminent technology decision, whereas BMD is not. Investing in BMD today promises ASAT dividends tomorrow, the hope being that BMD technologies will assist in the ASAT maturing process in such a way that Congress will vote for serial production and deployment as a classic bargaining chip. Secretary Weinberger's conversion to BMD complements his aversion to ASAT negotiations: he sees the two programs as inextricably linked in the effort to quietly seize the "high ground" of space and thereby regain military superiority.

The arms race in space promises to be exponentially more dangerous than the strategic posturing to date. History teaches us that the Soviet Union will respond to our space-based defensive systems in the same manner it has responded to our first generation of hydrogen bombs, MIRVs, and other strategic systems—with similar weapons and countervailing options of its own. Soviet experimentation with lasers and particle beams must not be ignored, and treaty violations must be strictly accounted for; but just as the earlier U.S. potential in ABM technology led to Soviet acquiescence (or ready acceptance, depending on how one reads Soviet policy) in the ABM Treaty of 1972, so can the current round of nascent defensive posturing lead to the effective demilitarization of space (demilitarization of offensive and threatening weapons in space, not communications or early-warning satellites).

The policy framework proposed here, then, builds upon the success of the ABM treaty arrangements worked out thus far and the most likely course of science and technology over the next several decades. It has become fashionable to deride the ABM Treaty of 1972, the major objection being that the Soviets do not actually believe in MAD and have struggled for more than a decade to break out of the treaty. Western strategists have argued for years on both sides of the issue, with many agreeing that the Soviet Union may be more than a bit schizophrenic in its adherence to MAD and its adherence to damage limitation where feasible. Limiting damage through BMD, however, may prove to be only marginally more effective than previous Soviet civil defense programs—the success of which is also the subject of much Western debate, primarily because there have been no opportunities to test their system realistically. In all probability, recent Soviet deployments will be viewed by the Soviet leadership as constituting a low-confidence defense at best. It would be imprudent, however, for the United States to assume that the USSR's BMD will necessarily be perceived as such in the Kremlin; other measures must be implemented to ensure that neither Moscow nor Washington could ever believe that BMD will be effective.

In 1983, the late Soviet leader Yuri Andropov proposed that ASAT and BMD programs be considered for treaty restrictions. Regardless of the initial unacceptability of the specifics of the Andropov proposal, the idea should be seized upon and made to fit into Western security goals. Soviet interest in new limitations implies a healthy respect for the potential of U.S. space operations. The advocates of BMD may be correct in asserting that the Soviet military will never accept MAD, but time and again they have been forced to live with it as the only reality extant or possible, however uncomfortable. American interest in a multilayered BMD and a qualitatively superior ASAT projectile has already engendered Soviet interest in negotiations, and the Soviet's respect for what they think we can do in the future is equally strong.

The time is ripe to pursue a two-tiered approach to offensive and defensive arms control that fits the emerging strategic environment of the 1990s and beyond. At the same time that we focus attention on reducing launcher limits and MIRV totals on all strategic forces (not just heavy, land-based ICBMs), we must also strive to reach an agreement that completely bans ASAT and BMD deployments based on earth, land, and sea, or in space. This may be done as an adjunct to the ABM Treaty of 1972, in which case Soviet resistance may be strong to a *total* ban on all ABM systems, or it may take the form of a new treaty allowing very limited, old-technology missile defense, with no provision for ASAT/BMD development or testing. The systems now being tested on both sides would be disallowed. Soviet refusal to negotiate on acceptable terms should not result in immediate U.S. ASAT or BMD deployments but should, instead, focus U.S. R&D into far less expensive countermeasures designed to frustrate any Soviet deployments. The effort must first be made, however, to explore all avenues toward banning the new generation of destabilizing space-theater weapons systems, wherever they are based.

Driven by fundamentally political or doctrinal motivations, the nuclear arms race has indeed become a race of technology, as posited by Edward Teller in 1980. The technologies themselves and the perceptions we accord to their presence (or their future development) are the primary tools with which the superpowers threaten, cajole, and ultimately deter one another from direct conflict. As a rational game, deterrence has always suffered from the unfortunate fact that people do not always react rationally. It would be even more foolhardy, however, to base our mutual relations on the premise that rationality will not prevail, for then no arrangement will be acceptable to either party. Given MAD, we have no choice but to make that reality work for us by forcing the strategic relationship into one of stable deterrence at increasingly lower levels of offensive arms. In the process, we will strengthen U.S. and international security for the next generation of strategic decision makers.

Notes

1. Sir Solly Zuckerman, *Scientists and War: The Impact of Science on Military and Civil Affairs*, 1967, p. 49.

2. Herbert York, *The Advisors: Oppenheimer, Teller, and the Superbomb*, 1976, pp. ix, 11.

3. Samuel Huntington, *The Common Defense: Strategic Programs in National Politics*, 1961, p. 285.

4. Ibid., p. 287. Huntington also writes (p. 298): "The innovation of the hydrogen bomb was the critical program in the emergence of a policy of strategic deterrence. It shaped the evolution of American strategy during the decade. Inevitably it led to long-range ballistic missiles, earth satellites, and space probes. It laid the basis for the nuclear stalemate of the 1950's and the resultant need for limited war forces."

5. Henry A. Kissinger, *Nuclear Weapons and Foreign Policy*, 1969, pp. 13–14.

6. Ibid., p. 170.

7. J.P. Ruina, "Aborted Military Systems," in Feld et al., eds., *Impact of New Technologies on the Arms Race*, 1971, p. 320; Warner R. Schilling, in "Scientists, Foreign Policy, and Politics," *American Political Science Review*, June 1962, p. 300, writes: "The contributions that science and technology will bring to international politics will largely turn, not so much on the particular arrangements of scientists in the policy-making process, but on the purposes of statesmen and the theories they have about the political world in which they live."

8. Colonel Richard G. Head, "Technology and the Military Balance," *Foreign Affairs*, April 1978, p. 554.

9. Albert Wohlstetter, "Strategy and the Natural Scientists," in Robert Gilpin and Christopher Wright, eds., *Scientists and National Policy-Making*, 1964, p. 178.

10. Bernard Baruch, *The Public Years*, 1960, p. 369.

11. Martin J. Sherwin, *A World Destroyed: The Atomic Bomb and the Grand Alliance*, 1973, p. 27.

12. Ibid.

13. Max Born, "Man and the Atom," *Bulletin of the Atomic Scientists*, June 1957, p. 593. Used with permission.

14. York, *The Advisors*, p. 22. He writes: "Thus, when Los Alamos was established, the exploration of the super was among the original objectives. However, because the development of fission bombs turned out to be more difficult than expected, their development demanded and received virtually the full attention of the laboratory. Only a relatively small group, under Teller's direction, put in much effort on the super during the war."

Hans Bethe's early work is discussed briefly in Robert Bacher, "The Hydrogen Bomb," *Bulletin of the Atomic Scientists*, May 1950, p. 134.

15. Arthur Compton, *Atomic Quest*, 1956, p. 127.

16. Teller lecture transcript, 1978, p. 15.

17. Compton, *Atomic Quest*, p. 128.

18. According to Teller (*The Legacy of Hiroshima,* 1962, p. 41), Oppenheimer told him "that we would not develop a hydrogen bomb" even before Nagasaki and the war's conclusion ("Memorandum for the Record," 18 August 1945, from the Manhattan Engineer District Records, Harrison-Bundy files, folder no. 98, National Archives, cited in Sherwin, *A World Destroyed*, Appendix Q, p. 315).

19. Dean Acheson, *Present at the Creation*, 1969, p. 346.

20. Hans Thirring, *Die Geschicte der Atombombe*, 1946, referred to in Thirring's March 1950 *Bulletin of the Atomic Scientists* article, "The Superbomb."

21. Testimony of Norris Bradbury, *In the Matter of J. Robert Oppenheimer: Transcript of Hearing Before the Personnel Security Board*, 1954, p. 484. When Luis Alvarez was asked if the super could have been developed sooner had a program been started earlier, he replied: "I think brilliant inventions come from a concentrated effort on a program. The reason there were not any brilliant inventions in the thermonuclear program for four years after the war is that there was no climate to develop in. Lots of people were not thinking about the program. Essentially one man was, and it is very hard to generate ideas in a vacuum" (Alvarez testimony, *In the Matter of . . . ,* p. 786).

22. York, *The Advisors*, pp. 23-24. The conferees felt it "appropriate to point out that further decision in a matter so filled with the most serious implications as is this one can properly be taken only as part of the highest national policy" (p. 24).

23. Bradbury, *In the Matter of . . . ,* p. 485. In further questioning by Dr. Gordon Gray, chairman of the AEC Personnel Security Board, Bradbury was asked: " . . . had there been a Presidential directive in 1945 or at some later date, perhaps, but earlier than January 1950, is it possible that we might have had the invention or discoveries earlier?" Bradbury replied: "My personal opinion in answer to that question is in the negative. . . . The only line of attack which had occurred to us on this problem throughout the years 1942 onwards seemed to be a line of attack during 1945-49 which would be frought with enormous technical difficulties, that is, practical technological difficulties" (Gray and Bradbury, *In the Matter of . . . ,* p. 487).

24. Bradbury, *In the Matter of . . . ,* p. 487.

25. The Strategic and Critical Materials Stockpiling Act of 1946, Public Law 520, 60 Stat. 596, cited in *The Foreign Relations of the United States:*

Vol. 1, National Security Affairs, Foreign Economic Policy, 1949–1950 (hereafter *FRUS*), 1975, p. 356 note.

26. Bradbury, *In the Matter of . . . ,* p. 493.

27. Luis Alvarez (a prominent University of California physicist), *In the Matter of . . . ,* p. 775.

28. George Orwell, "Politics and the English Language," in *A Collection of Essays,* 1953, p. 156.

29. Samuel Huntington recalls: "In November [1949], at the thirty-second anniversary of the revolution, the statements of Soviet leaders reached a new peak of truculence and hostility" (*The Common Defense,* p. 47). Daniel Yergin, in *Shattered Peace: The Origins of the Cold War and the National Security State,* 1977, cites Kennan's "long telegram" of 1946 (itself a reaction to Stalin's famous February 9 Bolshoi Theater speech) as the new "bible for American policymakers." News of the long telegram was purposely leaked in the United States "to dramatize the disputes among the Great Powers and push public opinion toward a state of alert" (Yergin, pp. 166, 170, 171).

30. This is one of the major themes of Yergin's book.

31. Warner R. Schilling, "The H-Bomb Decision: How to Decide Without Actually Choosing," *Political Science Quarterly,* No. 1, March 1961, p. 28.

32. Adam Ulam, *Expansion and Coexistence: The History of Soviet Foreign Policy,* 1968, p. 500.

33. *Survival in the Air Age: A Report by the President's Air Policy Commission,* 1948, p. 8.

34. Ibid., p. 14.

35. The discussion of Kennan's and the JCS's strategic plans follows Paul Y. Hammond, "SuperCarriers and B-36 Bombers: Appropriations, Strategy, and Politics," in Harold Stein, ed., *American Civil-Military Decisions,* 1963, pp. 503–504.

36. Huntington, *The Common Defense,* p. 48.

37. Zhores A. Medvedev, *Nuclear Disaster in the Urals,* 1979, p. 161.

38. Thucydides, *The Peloponnesian War* (trans. Rex Warner), 1977, p. 85.

39. Lewis L. Strauss, *Men and Decisions,* 1962, pp. 201–207.

40. Ibid., p. 207.

41. Harry Truman, *Memoirs: Years of Trial and Hope,* vol. 2, p. 309.

42. Testimony of Carroll Wilson before the JCAE, cited in Richard G. Hewlett and Francis Duncan, *Atomic Shield, 1947/1952: Vol. 2, A History of the United States Atomic Energy Commission,* 1969, p. 372.

43. Testimony of Lewis Strauss before the JCAE, in Hewlett and Duncan, *Atomic Shield,* p. 373.

44. Ibid., p. 374.

45. Strauss, *Men and Decisions*, pp. 216–217.

46. Testimony of David Lilienthal, *In the Matter of . . .* , p. 400. The AEC asked the GAC: "Is this program that we now have and have under way adequate to fulfill our duties? If not, what modification or what alternative course or alternative courses should be pursued? Among those alternative courses, should an all-out H-bomb program be instituted in order that we should adequately and properly fulfill our duty?" (Lilienthal, *In the Matter of . . .* , p. 400).

47. Diary of Luis Alvarez, October 5 entry, cited in Robert Jungk, *Brighter than a Thousand Suns: A Personal History of the Atomic Scientists* (trans. James Cleugh), 1958, p. 273.

48. Jungk, *Brighter than a Thousand Suns*, pp. 273–274.

49. Hewlett and Duncan, *Atomic Shield*, p. 377.

50. "President Truman to the Executive Secretary of the National Security Council [Soeurs]," Washington, July 26, 1949, in *FRUS 1949*, p. 502.

51. "Minutes of the 148th Meeting of the Policy Planning Staff, Tuesday, October 11, 1949, Department of State," in *FRUS 1949;* for Kennan's views, p. 402; for Acheson's, p. 403.

52. Huntington, *The Common Defense*, pp. 300–301.

53. Hewlett and Duncan, *Atomic Shield*, pp. 378–379; *In the Matter of . . .* , pp. 242–243.

54. Letter from Pike to Oppenheimer, October 21, 1949, in Hewlett and Duncan, *Atomic Shield*, p. 380.

55. Testimony of David Lilienthal, *In the Matter of . . .* , p. 399. On p. 400, Lilienthal states: "Among these parts [of the weapons improvement program] were a program for an increase in the numbers of atomic weapons through new design, an increase in the numbers of weapons through greater material production, an increase in the numbers of weapons through programs relating to raw materials, a program for increasing the destructive power of the weapons over those of Hiroshima and Nagasaki by a substantial factor, an improvement in the combat usefulness of the weapons by re-engineering these weapons. . . . And finally, plans for greatly stepped up power of weapons by a very large factor, by certain innovations of design that had been worked on for some time, but were at the point where a program for building such weapons was just around the corner. . . . I am assuming that this must be the fission bomb that was planned at the time of September 23."

56. Testimony of Isador I. Rabi, *In the Matter of . . .* , p. 456.

57. Thucydides, *The Peloponnesian War*, p. 84.

58. "The Chairman of the General Advisory Committee [Oppenheimer] to the Chairman of the United States Atomic Energy Commission (Lilienthal]," Washington, October 30, 1949, in *FRUS 1949*, p. 570.

59. Yergin, *Shattered Peace*, pp. 73–79.

60. Acheson, *Present at the Creation*, p. 345.

61. Hammond, "SuperCarriers," p. 504.

62. David Lilienthal, *The Journals of David E. Lilienthal: Vol. 2, The Atomic Energy Years 1945–1950*, 1964, entry of October 31, 1949, p. 583.

63. David S. McLellan, *Dean Acheson: The State Department Years*, 1976, pp. 177–178.

64. Hewlett and Duncan, *Atomic Shield*, p. 3.

65. Lilienthal, *Journals*, entry of October 30, 1949, p. 582.

66. Hewlett and Duncan, *Atomic Shield*, p. 383.

67. Ibid. See also "GAC Report of October 30, 1949," in York, *The Advisors*, p. 154.

68. All quotations in this paragraph (including the longer extract) are from "The Chairman of the General Advisory Committee [Oppenheimer] to the Chairman of the Atomic Energy Commission [Lilienthal]," Washington, October 30, 1949, in *FRUS 1949*, p. 571.

69. "An Opinion on the Development of the Super," Enclosure 2 of October 30 Oppenheimer memorandum (see note 68), in *FRUS 1949*, p. 572.

70. Lilienthal, *Journals*, entry of November 1, 1949, p. 583.

71. Hewlett and Duncan, *Atomic Shield*, p. 385.

72. Ibid., p. 388.

73. Ibid., p. 386.

74. "Minutes of a Meeting of the Policy Planning Staff, Department of State, November 3, 1949, 3 p.m.," in *FRUS 1949*, p. 574.

75. Ibid., pp. 575, 576.

76. For instance, compare this with Kennan, *Memoirs 1925–1950*, 1967, p. 475, where he writes of a "growing tendency in Washington" to plan on Soviet capabilities "and to exclude from consideration as something unsusceptible to exact determination, the whole question of that adversary's real intentions."

77. Lilienthal, *Journals*, entry of November 3, 1949, pp. 588–589.

78. Ibid., p. 589.

79. George F. Kennan, *Memoirs 1925–1950*, 1967, pp. 472–473.

80. Hewlett and Duncan, *Atomic Shield*, pp. 386–387.

81. Lilienthal, *Journals*, entry of November 6, 1949, p. 590.

82. Hewlett and Duncan, *Atomic Shield*, p. 389.

83. "The Chairman of the United States Atomic Energy Commission [Lilienthal] to President Truman—Enclosure—Memorandum for the President by the United States Atomic Energy Commission," Washington, November 9, 1949, in *FRUS 1949*, pp. 577–579.

84. Ibid., p. 580.

85. Ibid. The views of Lilienthal are on pp. 582–583; the view of Smyth on p. 584; the view of Dean on p. 583; and those of Dean and Strauss on p. 581.

86. Hewlett and Duncan, *Atomic Shield*, pp. 392–393.

87. Ibid., p. 393. In addition to Teller, Lawrence, and Alvarez, Dr. Karl T. Compton, a well-known physicist who contributed to the work of the Manhattan Project and who was, at the time of the hydrogen bomb debate, the chairman of the Defense Department's Research and Development Board, also urged the president to proceed with the super in a letter to Truman dated November 9, 1949. The letter is reproduced in Strauss, *Men and Decisions*, pp. 223–224.

88. "President Truman to the Executive Secretary of the National Security Council [Soeurs]," Washington, November 19, 1949, in *FRUS 1949*, p. 587.

89. "The Chairman of the Joint Committee on Atomic Energy [McMahon] to President Truman," Los Angeles, November 21, 1949, in *FRUS 1949*, pp. 588–589, 590–591, 594.

90. Ibid., p. 592.

91. Edward Teller and Allen Brown, *The Legacy of Hiroshima*, 1962, p. 45.

92. "Memorandum by the Joint Chiefs of Staff to the Secretary of Defense [Johnson]," Washington, November 23, 1949, in *FRUS 1949*, p. 595. See also Hewlett and Duncan, *Atomic Shield*, p. 395.

93. "Mr. Lewis L. Strauss, Member of the United States Atomic Energy Commission, to President Truman," Washington, November 25, 1949, in *FRUS 1949*, pp. 597–599.

94. "Memorandum by the Under Secretary of State [Webb]," Washington, December 3, 1949, in *FRUS 1949*, p. 600.

95. Ibid.

96. For all these views, see Hewlett and Duncan, *Atomic Shield*, p. 396.

97. Fine, "The Super," December 8, 1949, cited in Hewlett and Duncan, *Atomic Shield*, pp. 396–397.

98. Hewlett and Duncan, *Atomic Shield*, p. 397.

99. "Memorandum Circulated by the Defense Members of the Working Group of the Special Committee of the National Security Council," Washington, undated but prior to December 16, 1949, in *FRUS 1949*, pp. 606–610.

100. "Memorandum by the Deputy Director of the Policy Planning Staff [Nitze]," Washington, December 19, 1949, in *FRUS 1949*, p. 611.

101. For the views of Lilienthal, Johnson, and LeBaron, see Hewlett and Duncan, *Atomic Shield,* p. 398. At home on Christmas, Lilienthal observed: "It's now clear that sponsors of the H-bomb are scientists and military establishment, active and ardent." Lilienthal, *Journals,* Christmas Day entry, 1949, p. 614.

102. Acheson, *Present at the Creation*, p. 345; Hungtington, *The Common Defense*, p. 48.

103. McLellan, *Dean Acheson*, p. 177.

104. Roy A. Medvedev, *Let History Judge*, 1973, p. 479.

105. Ibid., p. 557.

106. F.D.R. (no date given), as quoted in Teller and Brown, p. 12.

107. Hewlett and Duncan, *Atomic Shield*, p. 399.

108. Ibid.

109. *Congress and the Nation, 1945–1964*, pp. 257–258.

110. James Reston, *New York Times*, January 17, 1950, p. 1.

111. "Memorandum by the Director of the Policy Planning Staff [Nitze] to the Secretary of State," Washington, January 17, 1950, in *FRUS 1950*, p. 13.

112. Hewlett and Duncan, *Atomic Shield*, p. 401.

113. Ibid., pp. 401–402: "McMahon dismissed the moral twinges as simply an emotional response to a difficult question. The nation would have to face the reality that 'total power in the hands of total evil will equal destruction.' "

114. Ibid., p. 403.

115. Acheson, *Present at the Creation*, p. 348.

116. Lilienthal, *Journals*, entry of January 26, 1950, pp. 620–621.

117. For the advice of the Weapons Systems Evaluation Group and McCormack, see Huntington, *The Common Defense*, p. 302; for the others, see Hewlett and Duncan, *Atomic Shield*, pp. 404–405.

118. Lilienthal, *Journals*, entry of January 28, 1950, p. 622. Lilienthal also noted that Urey's speech in New York "will stir up the animals."

119. Jungk, *Brighter than a Thousand Suns*, p. 284.

120. Lilienthal, *Journals*, entry of January 31, 1950, pp. 627–628; Hewlett and Duncan, *Atomic Shield,* pp. 406–407.

121. Lilienthal, *Journals*, p. 629.

122. Ibid., p. 630; Hewlett and Duncan, *Atomic Shield*, p. 407.

123. Lilienthal, *Journals*, p. 625.

124. Ibid., p. 626.

125. "Statement by the President on the Hydrogen Bomb," January 31, 1950, *Public Papers of the Presidents of the United States: Harry S. Truman, 1950*, p. 138.

126. Teller and Brown, p. 46.

127. Lilienthal, *Journals*, pp. 632–633; Margaret Truman, *Harry S. Truman*, 1973, p. 418; Harry Truman, *Memoirs*, p. 309.

128. Hewlett and Duncan, *Atomic Shield*, pp. 408–409.

129. "The President to the Secretary of State," Washington, January 31, 1950, in *FRUS 1950*, pp. 141–142.

130. *Congressional Record,* 81 Cong., 2 sess., February 2, 1950, pp. 1338–1340.

131. Hewlett and Duncan, *Atomic Shield*, p. 410.

132. "Draft Memorandum by the Counsellor [Kennan] to the Secretary of State," Washington, February 17, 1950, in *FRUS 1950*, p. 161.

133. Hewlett and Duncan, *Atomic Shield*, pp. 414–415.

134. "The Secretary of Defense [Johnson] to the President," Washington, February 24, 1950, in *FRUS 1950*, pp. 538–539.

135. "Report to the President by the Special Committee of the National Security Council on Development of Thermonuclear Weapons," no date but probably March 9, 1950, declassified March 30, 1976; Truman, *Memoirs*, p. 310.

136. Truman, *Memoirs*, pp. 311–312.

137. Ibid., p. 311; "Lay to the Secretaries of State, Defense, and the Chairman of the Atomic Energy Commission," March 10, 1950, Records of Headquarters, U.S. Atomic Energy Commission, Washington, D.C., cited in Hewlett and Duncan, *Atomic Shield*, p. 415.

138. Testimony of Hans Bethe, *In the Matter of . . .*, p. 330.

139. Enclosure 2, "A Report to the President Pursuant to the President's Directive of January 31, 1950," Washington, April 7, 1950, in *FRUS 1950*, p. 267.

140. Ibid., p. 268.

141. Huntington, *The Common Defense*, p. 54.

142. John Erickson, ed., *The Military Technical Revolution: Its Impact on Strategy and Foreign Policy*, 1966, p. 18.

143. Testimony of Edward Teller, *In the Matter of . . .*, p. 713.

144. Testimony of Hans Bethe, *In the Matter of . . .*, p. 330.

145. Edward Teller, "Back to the Laboratories," *Bulletin of the Atomic Scientists*, March 1950, pp. 71–72.

146. Testimony of Robert Oppenheimer, *In the Matter of . . .*, p. 81.

147. Ibid., p. 228.

148. Ibid., p. 18.

149. Harold P. Green and Alan Rosenthal, *Government of the Atom: The Integration of Powers*, 1963, p. 234.

150. Robert Gilpin, *American Scientists and Nuclear Weapons Policy*, 1962, p. 15; Gilpin further states: "We find the scientist who advises on nuclear weapons inevitably combining his scientific and his political judgment" (p. 16). Regarding the debate over the super, Gilpin writes: "The clash was between two opposed political views, and not between the politically motivated and the scientifically motivated" (p. 107).

151. Testimony of Edward Teller, *In the Matter of . . .*, p. 714. The same day Teller testified, Wendell Latimer (a chemist at the University of California, Berkeley) told the Personnel Security Board: "Granted at that time the odds of making a super weapon were not known, they talked about 50–50, 10 to 1, 100 to 1, but when the very existence of the Nation was involved, I didn't care what the odds were" (Latimer testimony, p. 659).

152. York, *The Advisors*, p. 27.

153. Testimony of Edward Teller, *In the Matter of . . .*, p. 718.

154. "Notes of the Interim Committee Meeting, May 31, 1945," cited in Sherwin, *A World Destroyed*, p. 297.

155. Schilling, "The H-Bomb Decision," p. 39.

156. McLellan, *Dean Acheson*, p. 177.

157. Truman, *Memoirs*, p. 307.

158. This is the essence of Schilling's "The H-Bomb Decision."

159. Eben A. Ayers diary, February 4, 1950.

160. *Seventh Semiannual Report of the Atomic Energy Commission, January 1950*, 1950, p. viii.

161. Ibid., p. 27.

162. "Report to the President on Development of Thermonuclear Weapons," March 9, 1950, p. 2.

163. Edward Teller, "Technology: The Imbalance of Power," in *The United States in the 1980s*, 1980, p. 518.

164. Montgomery of Alamein, *A History of Warfare*, p. 443.

165. Ibid., p. 447.

166. Jerome H. Kahan, *Security in the Nuclear Age*, 1975, p. 36.

167. Ibid., p. 37. Eugene Emme, in the editor's introduction to *The History of Rocket Technology*, 1964, briefly traced the historical antecedents of modern rocketry: "It was the military potential of rocket propulsion, an art lost to artillery in the 19th century, which created missilery as a strategic weapons system *and which brought forth the technology* making possible the birth of practical astronautics" (pp. 5–6, emphasis added). In a selection in Emme's book entitled "Early U.S. Satellite Proposals," R. Cargill Hall writes that, in many instances, "international rivalry . . . has frequently acted as *the* catalytic stimulus to technological advance" p. 67).

168. Michael Armacost, *The Politics of Weapons Innovation*, 1969, p. 258; and Adam Yarmolinsky, *The Military Establishment*, 1971, p. 109.

169. There does exist "the possibility that superheavy elements (as discussed by Dr. Olgaard) may exist and may have smaller critical mass and smaller weapon weight . . . but it is reasonable to suppose that even if these materials have properties which allow their use in practice (which is questionable) and costs which permit them to be considered at all (even less likely), they would not make an essentially important change in the existing situation." J. Carson Mark, "Nuclear Weapons Technology," in Feld et al., *Impact of New Technologies on the Arms Race*, 1971, p. 136. The reference to Dr. Olgaard relates to his article in the same book, entitled "On the Possible Military Significance of the Superheavy Elements," pp. 109–125.

170. Michael J. Deane, "Soviet Military Doctrine and Defensive Deployment Concepts: Implications for Soviet Ballistic Missile Defense," in Davis et al., *The Soviet Union and Ballistic Missile Defense*, 1980, p. 59.

Deane also notes that Richard Garwin and other physicists and engineers believe that "the chances of developing an effective charged-particle beam weapon are extremely remote. While acknowledging Soviet work in this area, they characterize Soviet efforts as 'completely irrelevant' and 'technically infeasible.' "

171. William Kincade, "Over the Technological Horizon," 1981. George Rathjens and Jack Ruina argue in the same issue of *Daedalus* that a leak-proof defensive system would be necessary to shift to an assured survival strategy, "and this cannot be done with any known technologies" ("Nuclear Doctrine and Rationality," p. 181).

172. Teller, "Technology," p. 514.

173. "DOD's Space-Based Program—Potential, Progress, and Problems," 1982, p. i.

174. "Pentagon Space Policy: More of the Same," *Aerospace Daily*, August 19, 1982, p. 279.

175. "DeLauer Questioned on US ASAT Work, Military Space Race," *Aerospace Daily*, September 21, 1982, p. 105.

176. *United States Military Posture for FY1983*, prepared by The Organization of the Joint Chiefs of Staff, 1982, p. 77.

177. *Report of the Secretary of Defense Caspar W. Weinberger to the Congress on the FY1984 Budget, FY1985 Authorization Request and FY1984–1988 Defense Programs*, February 1, 1983, pp. 227–228.

178. For a detailed exposition, see Daniel O. Graham, *High Frontier—A New National Strategy*, 1982. A synopsized description is offered in Daniel O. Graham, "High Frontier—A New National Strategy," in William J. Taylor, Jr., Steven A. Maaranen, and Gerrit W. Gong, eds., *Strategic Responses to Conflict in the 1980s*, 1983. Direct quotations in the text are taken from Graham's article in the Taylor et al. volume, pp. 839–851.

179. Ibid., p. 843. Graham further states that "a second generation space defense using more advanced technology can probably be achieved in the early 1990s."

180. Ibid., pp. 843, 847.

181. Patrick E. Tyler, "How Edward Teller Learned to Love the Nuclear-Pumped X-Ray Laser," *Washington Post*, April 3, 1983, p. D1.

182. Cited in Donald S. Harlacher, "High Frontier—A Strategy Based on Illusion," in Taylor et al., p. 863.

183. Ibid., p. 857.

184. Ibid., pp. 857–859.

185. Ibid., pp. 859–860. For the disruptive effects of electromagnetic pulse, see Daniel L. Stein, "Electromagnetic Pulse—The Uncertain Certainty," *Bulletin of the Atomic Scientists*, March 1983, pp. 52–56. Harlacher also discusses the solar power and space industrialization components of High Frontier, noting separate studies by the Office of Technology

Assessment, the National Academy of Sciences, and the National Research Council that cite development and operational costs higher by a factor of 300 and a timeframe greater by a factor of 6. Project concepts similar to High Frontier were "studied and restudied by the Department of Defense during the late 1970s and ultimately rejected due to several serious limitations," thus lending further credence to the notion that technology pull was not the determining factor in swaying the president and his closest advisors. Finally, William Kincade writes that High Frontier could well "lead to endless cost and . . . perhaps, a technological dead-end," and he points out that GBMD as presently conceived would not defend against depressed-trajectory submarine-launched ballistic missiles (SLBMs), bombers, or cruise missiles. See "Project High Frontier: Non-Technical Considerations," in Taylor et al., pp. 887–888.

186. Tyler, "How Edward Teller . . ." The Defense Department's view, as outlined in the second edition of *Soviet Military Power*, March 1983, was one of serious concern over Soviet progress. "Their high energy laser program is three-to-five times the US effort"; a space-based laser prototype system (initially as ASATs) could be emplaced as soon as the late 1980s; and orbital ABMs could be tested in the 1990s (pp. 68, 75).

187. Steven R. Weisman, "Reagan Proposes US Seek New Way to Block Missiles," *New York Times*, March 24, 1983, p. A21.

188. The White House, Office of the Press Secretary, press release of March 25, 1983.

189. "Hill Told of Breakthrough in Short Wavelength Laser Technology," *Aerospace Daily*, March 21, 1983, p. 117.

190. "Reagan Initiative Includes Cruise Missile Defense, Weinberger Says," *Aerospace Daily*, March 29, 1983, p. 161.

191. "Report of the President's Commission on Strategic Forces," April 1983, pp. 5, 9.

192. James B. Shultz, "Looking Realistically at Reagan's Space Plan," *Defense Electronics*, May 1983. Shultz wrote that the president's directive "will require technological breakthroughs on several fronts."

193. Clarence A. Robinson, Jr., "Panel Urges Defense Technology," *Aviation Week and Space Technology* (hereafter *AWST*), October 17, 1983, pp. 16–17.

194. Ibid., p. 18.

195. "Scientific Canvas Locates Innovative Defensive Ideas," *AWST*, October 17, 1983, p. 19.

196. Clarence A. Robinson, Jr., "Study Urges Exploiting of Technologies," *AWST*, October 24, 1983, p. 51.

197. Ibid., p. 55.

198. Ibid., p. 55. The Fletcher Report is much more optimistic about particle beams than Teller is. In his previously cited "Technology: The Im-

balance of Power," Teller wrote: "An extension in the range of particle beams has been widely predicted. But upon careful investigation, this development has proved so difficult technically that it is unpromising" (p. 531).

199. Ibid., p. 57.

200. Michael Feazel, "Europeans Support US Space-Based Systems," *AWST*, October 24, 1983, p. 59.

201. Clarence A. Robinson, Jr., "Shuttle May Aid in Space Weapons Test," *AWST*, October 31, 1983, p. 74.

202. Ibid., p. 77.

203. Ibid., p. 78.

204. Ibid.

205. Ibid.

206. Colin S. Gray, "Space Is Not a Sanctuary," *Survival*, September/October 1983, p. 198. Gray does not seem unduly optimistic about early breakthroughs in directed-energy weaponry as a potent system: unhardened Soviet SS-18s and SS-19s could be threatened in the 1990s "provided the Soviet Union did not effect such elementary counter-measures as rotating ICBM on launch or polishing booster skins," p. 199. It is difficult to imagine the USSR *not* taking these and other "elementary counter-measures."

207. Clarence A. Robinson, Jr., "Panel Urges Boost-Phase Intercepts," *AWST*, December 5, 1983, p. 50.

208. See John Steinbruner, "Launch Under Attack," *Scientific American*, January 1984, pp. 37–47, for an excellent discussion on the difficulty of coordinating retaliatory strikes under "dispersed control arrangements," even with a high degree of automated response. Policies such as launch under attack (LUA) or other measures that lead toward predelegation create an incentive to preempt an adversary's nuclear strike potential through early decapitation of his command-and-control apparatus—thus heightening crisis instability.

209. Robinson, "Panel Urges Boost-Phase Intercepts," pp. 51–52. The report acknowledges that the postboost reentry vehicles that survive the boost-phase intercept will vastly complicate the task of strategic defense.

210. Ibid., p. 61.

211. General Heiberg mentions the many problems ahead in developing target discrimination, sorting, and battle management, including command, control, communications, and intelligence (C^3I) functions. See Jack Cushman, "Wanted: New ABM Missile," *Defense Week*, August 8, 1983, p. 5. Under Secretary of Defense Richard DeLauer warned against undue optimism in the pages of *Aviation Week* itself: "There are big questions about space-based radars" ("Military Cautious on Space Station Role," *AWST*, July 25, 1983, p. 21).

212. "USAF Studies Hypervelocity Technology," *AWST*, December 5, 1983, pp. 62, 64.

213. Ibid., p. 68.

214. Harold Brown, Secretary of Defense, *Department of Defense Annual Report to the Congress, Fiscal Year 1981*, January 29, 1980, p. 136.

215. Morton H. Halperin, *Bureaucratic Politics and Foreign Policy*, 1974, p. 309.

216. Ibid., p. 24.

217. "Soviet Antimissile Lead is Feared," *New York Times*, December 5, 1983, p. A4.

218. Cited in Charles Mohr, "Reagan Is Urged to Increase Research on Exotic Defenses Against Missiles," *New York Times*, November 5, 1983, p. 32.

219. Ibid. Several unnamed administration officials said that the technologies under consideration were so "immature" that affixing a production price tag would be "difficult."

220. Cited in Jack Cushman, "Beam Weapon Advances Foretell Revolution in Strategic Warfare," *Defense Week*, September 12, 1983, p. 10.

221. Robert M. Bowman, "Star Wars: Pie in the Sky," *New York Times*, December 14, 1983, p. A35.

222. "Bill Supports Missile Defense," *AWST*, November 21, 1983, p. 22. Senator Armstrong's bill, S. 2021, is entitled "A Bill to Implement the Call of the President for a National Strategy Seeking to Protect People from Nuclear War and to Render Nuclear Weapons Obsolete" and is known as the People Protection Act. The bill was introduced in the Senate on October 28, 1983. See *Congressional Record*, October 28, 1983, p. S14840.

223. Caspar W. Weinberger, Secretary of Defense, *Annual Report to the Congress, FY1985*, Washington: U.S. GPO, February 1, 1984. For National Security Decision Directive (NSDD) 119, see "Washington Roundup," *AWST*, January 30, 1984, p. 15.

224. Ashton B. Carter, "BMD Applications: Performance and Limitations," in Ashton B. Carter and David N. Schwartz, eds., *Ballistic Missile Defense*, Washington, DC: The Brookings Institution, 1984, p. 118.

225. Kosta Tsipis, "Laser Weapons," *Scientific American*, December 1981, p. 52.

226. Ibid., p. 54.

227. Daniel Kaplan, "Lasers for Missile Defense," *Bulletin of the Atomic Scientists*, May 1983, p. 5.

228. The numbers and examples follow Tsipis, "Laser Weapons," p. 55.

229. Ibid. It should be stressed, again, that geosynchronous orbit is desirable because "the lower the orbit and range of a laser, the smaller the

area of the laser's coverage'' (see Kaplan, ''Lasers for Missile Defense,'' p. 5). It also follows, however, that the power levels necessary to generate such tremendous pulses or waves are far greater at 22,300 miles (about 36,000 kilometers) than at 625 miles (about 1,000 kilometers), the range cited in the examples in the text.

230. Kaplan, ''Lasers for Missile Defense,'' p. 6. A 4-meter-diameter mirror reflecting the power of a 100 megawatt hydrogen-fluoride laser would only require 1 second to destroy an ICBM, but such a large mirror is currently well beyond the capabilities of the United States or other countries: ''There are scant prospects for constructing an optically precise four-meter mirror'' (Tsipis, ''Laser Weapons,'' p. 55).

231. Tsipis, ''Laser Weapons,'' p. 55.

232. Schultz, ''Looking Realistically.''

233. Kaplan, ''Lasers for Missile Defense,'' p. 6.

234. Tsipis, ''Laser Weapons,'' p. 56.

235. Ibid. Tsipis calculates that a 100-megawatt hydrogen-fluoride laser—the construction of which is seriously doubted—will need 660 kilograms of fuel for each ICBM kill. At 1,000 ICBMs, 660 metric tons of fuel are required for each station. (Each station must be able to destroy the entire fleet of Soviet ICBMs in a minimal, 50 station deployment.) That fuel requirement necessitates about twenty shuttle loads. With fifty stations, 1,000 shuttle flights *for fuel alone* must occur (20 × 50). If our four shuttles would dedicate two flights per year each to fuel shipments alone, 125 years would elapse before the stations were fully fueled.

236. Cited in ''The New Arms Race: Star Wars Weapons,'' Union of Concerned Scientists Briefing Paper #5, October 1983.

237. See Tsipis, ''Laser Weapons,'' pp. 56–57, and Kaplan, ''Lasers for Missile Defense,'' pp. 6–7.

238. Kaplan, ''Lasers for Missile Defense,'' p. 6.

239. From conversations with numerous physicists and engineers. I would particularly like to note the comments of Professor Daniel L. Stein of the Princeton University Department of Physics.

240. Cited in Gray, ''Space Is Not a Sanctuary,'' p. 201.

241. Ibid. The five additional treaties not listed in the text are the International Telecommunications Convention, the Hot-Line Modernization Agreement of 1971, SALT I, the Convention on Registration of Objects Launched into Outer Space of 1975, and SALT II, which is signed but not ratified by the U.S. government. Both the United States and the USSR have agreed to abide by the terms of SALT II for the present.

242. Jack Ruina, ''ABM Revisited: Promise or Peril?'' *Washington Quarterly*, Autumn 1981, p. 65.

243. David Holloway, summarizing the views of Matthew Gallagher and Arthur J. Alexander, in ''Doctine and Technology in Soviet Armaments

Policy,'' in Derek Leebaert, ed., *Soviet Military Thinking*, 1981, p. 260. Those views were in reference to the Soviet weapons acquisiton process, but they apply equally well to the United States. Holloway mentions the "widely held belief that . . . in the USA technology drives doctrine," whereas the reverse supposedly holds true in the USSR. He finds that doctrinal "require-ments do play a key role in stimulating innovation and in giving direction" in the Soviet military R&D process, but he notes the strong bureaucratic push from the large R&D establishment in generating new weapons designs and projects (pp. 283, 286).

244. Cited in Daniel Deudney, "The Star Wars Scenario," *Baltimore Sun*, December 4, 1983, p. K-1.

245. Fred Hiatt, "Limited ABM is Urged To Protect U.S. Missiles," *Washington Post*, March 8, 1984, p. 30.

246. Ibid.

Bibliography

Memoirs and Personal Accounts

Acheson, Dean. *Present at the Creation*. New York: Norton, 1969.

Ayers, Eben A. Unpublished diary. Harry S. Truman Library, Independence, Mo.

Baruch, Bernard. *The Public Years*. New York: Holt, Rhinehart and Winston, 1960.

Kennan, George F. *Memoirs 1925–1950*. Boston and Toronto: Little, Brown, 1967.

Lilienthal, David E. *The Journals of David E. Lilienthal: Vol. 2. The Atomic Energy Years 1945–1950*. New York, Evanston, and London: Harper & Row, 1964.

Montgomery, Bernard Law (First Viscount Montgomery of Alamein). *A History of Warfare*. Cleveland: World Publishing Co., 1968.

Strauss, Lewis L. *Men and Decisions*. Garden City, N.Y.: Doubleday, 1962.

Teller, Edward. Photocopied transcript of unpublished October 1978 lecture.

Teller, Edward, and Brown, Allen. *The Legacy of Hiroshima*. Garden City, N.Y.: Doubleday, 1962.

Truman, Harry S. *Memoirs: Vol. 2. Years of Trial and Hope*. Garden City, N.Y.: Doubleday, 1956.

Truman, Margaret. *Harry S. Truman*. New York: Morrow, 1973.

Government Documents

Congress and the Nation 1945–1964. Washington, D.C.: U.S. Government Printing Office, 1965.

Congressional Record. 81 Cong. 2 sess., February 2, 1950.

Department of Defense Annual Report to the Congress, Fiscal Year 1985. Washington, D.C.: U.S. Government Printing Office, February 1, 1984.

"DOD's Space-Based Program—Potential, Progress, and Problems." Report by the Comptroller General of the United States (MASAD-82-10). Washington, D.C.: U.S. General Accounting Office, February 26, 1982.

The Foreign Relations of the United States, Vol. 1, National Security Affairs, Foreign Economic Policy, 1949–1950. Washington, D.C.: U.S. Government Printing Office, 1976 and 1977.

In the Matter of J. Robert Oppenheimer: Transcript of Hearing Before Personnel Security Board. Washington, D.C.: U.S. Government Printing Office, 1954.

Public Papers of the Presidents of the United States: Harry S. Truman, 1950. Washington, D.C., U.S. Government Printing Office, 1965.

"Report to the President by the Special Committee of the National Security Council on Development of Thermonuclear Weapons." Papers of Harry S. Truman, President's Secretary's Files, Harry S. Truman Library, Independence, Mo.

Seventh Semiannual Report of the Atomic Energy Commission, January 1950. Washington, D.C.: U.S. Government Printing Office, 1950.

Survival in the Air Age: A Report by the President's Air Policy Commission. Washington, D.C.: U.S. Government Printing Office, 1948.

Books and Articles

Allison, Graham T., and Morris, Frederic A. "Armaments and Arms Control: Exploring the Determinants of Military Weapons." *Daedalus 104,* Summer 1975.

Armacost, Michael. *The Politics of Weapons Innovation: The Thor-Jupiter Controversy.* New York and London: Columbia University Press, 1969.

Bacher, Robert. "The Hydrogen Bomb," *Bulletin of the Atomic Scientists 6,* May 1950.

Born, Max. "Man and the Atom." *Bulletin of the Atomic Scientists*, June 1957.

Brooks, Harvey. "The Military Innovation System and the Qualitative Arms Race." *Daedalus*, Summer 1975.

Carter, Ashton B. "BMD Applications: Performance and Limitations." In Ashton B. Carter and David N. Schwartz, eds., *Ballistic Missile Defense.* Washington, D.C.: Brookings, 1984.

Compton, Arthur Holly. *Atomic Quest.* New York: Oxford University Press, 1956.

Deane, Michael J. "Soviet Military Doctrine and Defensive Deployment Concepts: Implications for Soviet Ballistic Missile Defense." In Jacquelyn K. Davis, Robert L. Pfaltzgraff, Jr., Uri Ra'anan, Michael J. Deane, and John M. Collins, *The Soviet Union and Ballistic Missile Defense.* Cambridge, Mass.: Institute for Foreign Policy Analysis, March 1980.

Emme, Eugene, ed. *The History of Rocket Technology: Essays on Research, Development, and Utility.* Detroit: Wayne State University Press, 1964.

Erickson, John, ed. *The Military Technical Revolution: Its Impact on Strategy and Foreign Policy.* New York: Praeger, 1966.

Feld, B.T.; Greenwood, T.; Rathjens, G.W.; and Weinberg, S. *Impact of New Technologies on the Arms Race.* Cambridge, Mass.: MIT Press, 1971.

Gilpin, Robert. *American Scientists and Nuclear Weapons Policy.* Princeton: Princeton University Press, 1962.

Gilpin, Robert, and Wright, Christopher. *Scientists and National Policy-Making.* New York and London: Columbia University Press, 1964.

Graham, Daniel O. *High Frontier—A New National Strategy.* Washington, D.C.: Heritage Foundation, 1982.

_____ . "High Frontier—A New National Strategy." In William J. Taylor, Jr., Steven A. Maaranen, and Gerrit W. Gong, eds., *Strategic Responses to Conflict in the 1980s.* Washington, D.C.: Center for Strategic and International Studies, 1983. (To be published by Lexington Books in 1984.)

Gray, Colin S. "Space Is Not a Sanctuary." *Survival,* September/October 1983.

Green, Harold P., and Rosenthal, Alan. *Government of the Atom: The Integration of Powers.* New York: Atherton Press, 1963.

Halperin, Morton H. *Bureaucratic Politics and Foreign Policy.* Washington, D.C.: Brookings, 1974.

Hammond, Paul Y. "SuperCarriers and B-36 Bombers: Appropriations, Strategy, and Politics." In Harold Stein, ed., *American Civil-Military Decisions.* University: University of Alabama Press, 1963.

Head, Colonel Richard G. "Technology and the Military Balance." *Foreign Affairs 56,* April 1978.

Hewlett, Richard G., and Duncan, Francis. *Atomic Shield, 1947/1952: Vol. 2. A History of the United States Atomic Energy Commission.* University Park and London: Pennsylvania State University Press, 1969.

Holloway, David. "Doctrine and Technology in Soviet Armaments Policy." In Derek Leebaert, ed., *Soviet Military Thinking.* London: George Allen and Unwin, 1981.

Huntington, Samuel P. *The Common Defense: Strategic Programs in National Politics.* New York and London: Columbia University Press, 1961.

Jungk, Robert. *Brighter Than a Thousand Suns: A Personal History of the Atomic Scientists* (trans. James Cleugh). New York: Harcourt, Brace and World, 1958.

Kahan, Jerome H. *Security in the Nuclear Age.* Washington, D.C.: Brookings, 1975.

Kaplan, Daniel. "Lasers for Missile Defense." *Bulletin of the Atomic Scientists,* May 1983.

Kincade, William. "Over the Technological Horizon." *Daedalus,* Winter 1981, pp. 117, 120–120.

_____ . "Project High Frontier: Non-Technical Considerations." In William J. Taylor, Jr., Steven A. Maaranen, and Gerrit W. Gong, eds., *Strategic Responses to Conflict in the 1980s.* Washington, D.C.: Center for Strategic and International Studies, 1983. (To be published by Lexington Books in 1984.)

Kissinger, Henry A. *Nuclear Weapons and Foreign Policy*. New York: Norton, 1969.

McLellan, David S. *Dean Acheson: The State Department Years*. New York: Dodd, Mead, 1976.

Medvedev, Roy A. *Let History Judge* (trans. Colleen Taylor). New York: Vintage Books, 1973.

Medvedev, Zhores A. *Nuclear Disaster in the Urals* (trans. George Saunders). New York: Vintage Books, 1979.

Orwell, George. *A Collection of Essays*. New York: Harcourt Brace Jovanovich, 1953.

Ruina, J.P. "Aborted Military Systems." In B.T. Feld, T. Greenwood, G.W. Rathjens, and S. Weinberg, eds., *Impact of New Technologies on the Arms Race*. Cambridge, Mass.: MIT Press, 1971.

Ruina, Jack. "ABM Revisited: Promise or Peril?" *Washington Quarterly*, Autumn 1981, p. 65.

Ruina, Jack, and Rathjens, George. "Nuclear Doctrine and Rationality." *Daedalus*, Winter 1981, p. 181.

Schilling, Warner R. "The H-Bomb Decision: How To Decide Without Actually Choosing." *Political Science Quarterly*, March 1961.

———. "Scientists, Foreign Policy, and Politics." *American Political Science Review 54*, June 1962.

Schilling, Warner R.; Hammond, Paul Y.; and Snyder, Glenn H. *Strategy, Politics, and Defense Budgets*. New York and London: Columbia University Press, 1962.

Sherwin, Martin J. *A World Destroyed: The Atomic Bomb and the Grand Alliance*. New York: Vintage Books, 1973.

Snow, C.P. *Science and Government*. Cambridge, Mass.: Harvard University Press, 1961.

Stein, Daniel L. "Electromagnetic Pulse—The Uncertain Certainty." *Bulletin of the Atomic Scientists*, March 1983, pp. 52–56.

Steinbruner, John. "Launch Under Attack." *Scientific American*, January 1984, pp. 37–47.

Taylor, William J., Jr.; Maaranen, Steven A.; and Gong, Gerrit W., eds. *Strategic Responses to Conflict in the 1980s*. Washington, D.C.: Center for Strategic and International Studies, 1983. (To be published by Lexington Books in 1984.)

Teller, Edward. "Back to the Laboratories." *Bulletin of the Atomic Scientists*, March 1950, pp. 71–72.

———. "Technology: The Imbalance of Power." In Peter Duignan and Alvin Rabushka, eds., *The United States in the 1980s*. Stanford, Calif.: Hoover Institution Press, 1980.

Thirring, Hans. "The Superbomb." *Bulletin of the Atomic Scientists 6*, March 1950.

Thucydides. *The Peloponnesian War* (trans. Rex Warner). New York: Penguin Books, 1977.

Tsipis, Kosta. "Laser Weapons." *Scientific American*, December 1981.

Tyler, Patrick E. "How Edward Teller Learned to Love the Nuclear-Pumped X-Ray Laser." *Washington Post*, April 3, 1983, p. D1.

Ulam, Adam B. *Expansion and Coexistence: The History of Soviet Foreign Policy*. New York: Praeger, 1968.

Weisman, Steven R. "Reagan Proposes US Seek New Way to Block Missiles." *New York Times*, March 24, 1983.

Wohlstetter, Albert. "Strategy and the Natural Scientists." In Robert Gilpin and Christopher Wright, *Scientists and National Policy-Making*. New York and London: Columbia University Press, 1964.

Yarmolinsky, Adam. *The Military Establishment*. New York: Harper & Row, 1971.

Yergin, Daniel. *Shattered Peace: The Origins of the Cold War and the National Security State*. Boston: Houghton Mifflin, 1977.

York, Herbert. *The Advisors: Oppenheimer, Teller, and the Superbomb*. San Francisco: W.H. Freeman, 1976.

Zuckerman, Solly. *Scientists and War: The Impact of Science on Military and Civil Affairs*. New York and Evanston: Harper & Row, 1967.

Index

About the Author

Jonathan B. Stein is a legislative assistant to U.S. Senator Paul Simon. Before joining Senator Simon's staff, he was a Fellow at the Center for Strategic and International Studies. His first book, *The Soviet Bloc, Energy and Western Security,* was published by Lexington Books in 1983.

Mr. Stein received a B.A. in political science from Vassar College in 1979 and an M.S. in foreign service from the Georgetown University School of Foreign Service in 1981. He was a federal summer intern in 1980 covering the Warsaw Pact states in the Office of International Security Affairs, within the Office of the Secretary of Defense.